Transcendental Spirituality, Wisdom and Virtue

Our religious beliefs, despite predictions that they would disappear from our lives, continue to play an important part in contemporary society. Religious faith provides society with cohesion and solidarity and a sense of community through shared beliefs, together with social influence which promotes moral, ethical and empathetic behavior in society. More importantly, it offers meaning and purpose in answering existential questions, particularly in a pandemic environment, with many of us now thinking about our mortality. Yet there are distressing consequences arising from differing religious beliefs and practices as evidenced by the countless wars and conflicts that have had an overt or covert religious dimension throughout history and increasingly to the present day. Sadly, today we live in a time of increasing prejudice and persecution with the followers of most major religions reporting increasing hostility and, in many cases, violence. What the author has achieved in *Transcendental Spirituality, Wisdom and Virtue: The Divine Virtues and Treasures of the Heart*, through an extensive comparative listing of each of the universal principles and divine virtues, is to show the reader that regardless of the origin of our beliefs, the sacred scriptures provide us universally with wisdom, holiness, inspiration and spiritual nourishment. Clearly the author has achieved a primary objective in writing by assisting readers to reflect on their own spirituality and faith but more importantly to understand and appreciate the spiritual unity across our individual beliefs. At no time in history has it been more important to take time to learn about our neighbors' culture and beliefs. This book will greatly assist us in commencing this important journey.

Professor Philip Evans, the University of Notre Dame Australia

Love and kindness are a fundamental part of all religions. Douglas Hodgson has drawn upon many inspirational quotations from different religious teachings within his book to help us understand and appreciate the similarities between these traditions. *Transcendental Spirituality, Wisdom and Virtue: The Divine Virtues and Treasures of the Heart* is an inspirational book.

Thupten Lodey, Buddhist Bikshu

For many years, the Holy Grail of Religious Studies has been an explanation of common foundations of the world's great religions. No consensus has yet emerged, but Douglas Hodgson has brought fresh insight to the issue. Bringing a unique set of skills including legal studies and human rights, Hodgson brings much needed clarity to the question of the spiritual and ethical principles common to the world's faiths. In addition, he goes beyond the "Ivory Tower" to help explain how all people of goodwill can apply these principles to everyday life. I highly recommend the book.

Professor Matthew Ogilvie, former Dean of the School of Philosophy and Theology, the University of Notre Dame Australia

Transcendental Spirituality, Wisdom and Virtue

The Divine Virtues and Treasures of the Heart

Transcendental Spirituality, Wisdom and Virtue

The Divine Virtues and Treasures of the Heart

Douglas Charles Hodgson

Winchester, UK
Washington, USA

JOHN HUNT PUBLISHING

First published by O-Books, 2023
O-Books is an imprint of John Hunt Publishing Ltd., 3 East St., Alresford,
Hampshire SO24 9EE, UK
office@jhpbooks.com
www.johnhuntpublishing.com
www.o-books.com

For distributor details and how to order please visit the 'Ordering' section on our website.

ISBN: 978 1 80341 143 9
978 1 80341 144 6 (ebook)
Library of Congress Control Number: 2022900842

A CIP catalogue record for this book is available from the British Library.

Design: Matthew Greenfield

UK: Printed and bound by CPI Group (UK) Ltd, Croydon, CR0 4YY
Printed in North America by CPI GPS partners

We operate a distinctive and ethical publishing philosophy in
all areas of our business, from our global network of authors to
production and worldwide distribution.

Contents

Preface   1

Chapter 1: Introduction   3
Chapter 2: Absence of Anger and Bitterness   11
Chapter 3: Absence of Covetousness,
    Greed and Envy   15
Chapter 4: Absence of Enmity, Hatred and a
    Desire for Revenge   20
Chapter 5: Absence of Stealing   23
Chapter 6: Austerity   26
Chapter 7: Belief in One God (Monotheism/the
    Oneness of God)   29
Chapter 8: Charity and Service   40
Chapter 9: Compassion (Humanity)   47
Chapter 10: Conscience   52
Chapter 11: Detachment (from the Material World)   54
Chapter 12: Devotional Prayer (Worship) and Piety   64
Chapter 13: Faith   75
Chapter 14: Fearlessness (Courage)   82
Chapter 15: Fear of God (Reverential Awe/Wonder)   86
Chapter 16: Forgiveness (Mercy) and Reconciliation   89
Chapter 17: Fortitude (Steadfastness in
    Faith/Spiritual Knowledge)   93
Chapter 18: Gentleness (Lenity)   97
Chapter 19: The Golden Rule (Reciprocity
    or Mutuality)   101
Chapter 20: Humility (Absence of Pride and Vanity)   104
Chapter 21: Living in the Present Moment
    (Contemplative Mindfulness)   112
Chapter 22: Loving-Kindness (Benevolence)   116

Chapter 23: Natural Environment
    (Respect and Reverence for)   121
Chapter 24: Non-Judgmental Disposition (Absence
    of Fault-Finding)   127
Chapter 25: Non-Violence/Non-Injury
    (Prohibition of Killing)   132
Chapter 26: Patience (Forbearance)   136
Chapter 27: Peacefulness (Equanimity)
    and Contentment   141
Chapter 28: Purity (Holiness)   148
Chapter 29: Quietude   154
Chapter 30: Repentance and Atonement   158
Chapter 31: Restraint (Self-Control/Moderation)
    of the Senses   164
Chapter 32: Righteousness   176
Chapter 33: Simplicity   184
Chapter 34: Study of the Sacred Scriptures   188
Chapter 35: Truthfulness   191
Chapter 36: Understanding (Knowledge)   197
Chapter 37: Wisdom   202
Chapter 38: Conclusion   210

Author Biography   216
Bibliography   218

Dedicated to, and in high praise, thanksgiving and awe of, the
One and Only True God, Creator of all that exists,
Bestower of all life and Lord of Infinity.

Other Books Written by this Author

The Human Right to Education
(Dartmouth/Ashgate, Aldershot, England, 1998)
ISBN: 978-1-85521-909-3

Individual Duty within a Human Rights Discourse
(Ashgate, Aldershot, England, 2003)
ISBN: 978-0-7546-2361-8

The Law of Intervening Causation
(Ashgate, Aldershot, England, 2008)
ISBN: 978-0-7546-7366-8

International Human Rights and Justice
(Nova Science Publishers, Inc., New York, NY, USA, 2016)
(Editor)
ISBN: 978-1-63484-709-4

The human mystery is incredibly demeaned by scientific reductionism...we have to recognize that we are spiritual beings with souls existing in a spiritual world as well as material beings with bodies and brains existing in a material world.

Sir John Eccles

Preface

In these times differences and divisions appear to consume us on a daily basis. In a post-secular and increasingly technological and digitized world which is now exploring possibilities in Artificial Intelligence, ancient wisdom and virtue appear to have been cast aside as unfashionable and irrelevant. As knowledge exponentially increases, application of the wisdom of the elders recedes. But why must this be so? Can we not explore and affirm what unites and binds humanity together, and what has brought us to this point in human history?

I have therefore searched the sacred scriptures of the most prominent religions and belief systems with a view to determining not what divides or differentiates them but to identify and celebrate the common spiritual and ethical foundations upon which they are all based. It is my hope that readers who consider themselves spiritual and/or religious, those who are interested in interfaith dialogue and those who may still be searching for their own truth will be able to identify with and embrace in their lives the Divine Virtues and Universal Ethical Principles which bind these religions together like an ethereal mortar. This book's trinity of purpose is to assist readers to identify with and elevate their own spirituality, to better understand their own religion or faith through a spiritual prism, and to encourage them to better understand and appreciate the spiritual and ethical unity underlying the world's religions.

Transcendental Spirituality, Wisdom and Virtue: The Divine Virtues and Treasures of the Heart draws upon remarkably similar universal ethical principles which underpin the world's faiths to provide a platform for personal growth and spiritual wealth, and a guide to how we can better relate to others and the natural environment in our daily activities. It identifies and explains the meaning of 36 Divine Virtues which form the foundation of the world's great religions, traced back to a single Source unifying and connecting all, and reveals in a practical way how ancient virtue and wisdom may be applied in today's increasingly complex and challenging world to provide sanctuary, comfort, meaning, contentment and a return to simplicity.

This is a reminder to humanity to return to the Source of all that is. It is not yet too late. Ancient virtues and wisdom are just as relevant and important today as they have ever been.

I would like to express my deep and abiding gratitude to the Powers and Principalities, the Archangels and Ascended Masters who inspired and guided me in the writing of this book, a gift and offering to *Om*. My role was confined to that of scribe.

Douglas Hodgson

Chapter 1

Introduction

Religions have developed as a Divinely-inspired guide to ethical and moral conduct. They form an integral and fundamental part of many people's lives, providing guidance, hope and comfort. However, religions and their mutual rivalries and missionary zeal, which have at times proven historically to be divisive, leading to both inter-religious and intra-religious strife and the spillage of blood in the name of righteousness, are perhaps of less consequence than the common and unifying spiritual principles and virtues upon which they are based. Having preceded all religion, God is of no religion; yet His spiritual essence is the source of all religion.

Twelve religions and belief systems – Baha'i, Buddhism (including Zen Buddhism), Christianity, Confucianism, Hinduism, indigenous spiritual beliefs, Islam, Jainism, Judaism, Sikhism, Taoism and Zoroastrianism – have evolved from various common underlying or foundational spiritual principles. Some 36 such shared Divine Virtues or Universal Principles have been identified. They represent the heart and soul, the spirit and essence, indeed the source of these religions and belief systems. This Source of spirituality is one and the same in origin to all, as God is One but common to all these faiths. These faiths and religions all contain the same eternal spiritual truths though they may be expressed in slightly different and nuanced ways, due to varying historical, cultural, anthropological and social circumstances.

These Universal Principles and Divine Virtues merit our greater scrutiny and respect as the substance of mainstream religions and belief systems has drawn heavily on these underlying spiritual tenets. It is useful, indeed necessary, therefore, to identify and expound the fundamental spiritual principles and virtues upon which the mainstream religions are founded. As will become apparent to the reader, various religions from all parts of the world appear to converge on what is essentially one and the same God/Source and Divine Law. A common and interconnected spiritual cord unites all of humanity. It is hoped that the mutually reinforcing and parallel spiritual norms and virtues mentioned in the scriptural passages referenced in this book will assist in unifying people, at least those of faith, who must increasingly navigate a divided and fractious world.

Ignorance (in the sense of unconscious separation from God and the reality of His unconditional and unlimited love for us) emanates from an excessive immersion in worldly material illusions. Most people never really reflect on their existence and the deeper meaning of life or the pristine Source of virtue and goodness. What is proposed is the cultivation and implementation of the Divine Virtues and Laws of the Heart into our daily lives so that resort to them supersedes our innate, base and reactive instincts in our daily interactions, thereby spiritually elevating ourselves. The goal is to strive for purification, initiated by us and assisted by the Divine, enabling us to live a more upright, enlightened and wholesome life; to perceive and appreciate the Ultimate Reality or the way things really are, rather than being trapped in our pursuit of self-preoccupied ambitions and worldly illusions.

The format of this book is to devote one chapter to each Divine Virtue. Each chapter is prefaced by a Commentary which attempts to explain the meaning, scope and reach of the Divine Virtue drawn from supporting scriptural references which are the source of the particular Divine Virtue. Where appropriate and considered useful to supplement the discussion of the meaning of various Divine Virtues, limited references have also been made to the writings of individual authors, such as Mohandas

4

Gandhi (Hinduism), His Holiness The Dalai Lama (Buddhism) and the anonymous author of the *Desiderata* (Christianity).

This book is essentially devoted to the articulation of ancient interfaith Divine wisdom and knowledge, timeless in nature and operation and impervious to the ebb and flow of human thought and fashion, arguably as relevant today as in any previous era in human history as we continue to face continuing existential threats to the survival of humanity. Its primary objectives are as follows:

- To assist readers to identify with, and elevate, their own spirituality or consciousness through reflection upon how they may better cultivate and implement the Divine Virtues in their daily living by relying on them as a sound reference-point.
- To assist readers to better understand their own religion or faith through a spiritual prism, and to better understand and appreciate God's qualities and attributes (and thereby draw closer to God).
- To encourage readers to better understand and appreciate the spiritual unity across the various faith and belief systems.

Whatever your faith and whatever you conceive God to be, the Holy Scriptures reveal the mind, qualities and attributes of God. May these Divine Virtues and supporting scriptural references provide to readers wisdom, holiness, treasures of the heart, light, inspiration, spiritual nourishment and a ladder to the ascending heavens. You will discover that your real treasures, the ones that will guide you through this earthly life, reside in your heart and that virtue has both a heavenly and its own earthly reward. For where your treasure is, there will your heart be also (Matthew chapter 6 verse 21).

Scriptural References

Baha'i
Ascend to that for which you were created.

(Of Divine Humanity: Words of Wisdom from the Supreme Pen of Baha'u'llah)

Buddhism
Few...are they who arrive at the other shore (attain enlightenment). The others merely run up and down the shore of this side (this world).

(The Dhammapada chapter 6 (The Wise Man) verse 85)

To dwell on the highest thoughts (devote oneself to higher consciousness), this is the teaching of the Awakened.

(The Dhammapada chapter 14 (The Buddha/The Awakened) verse 185)

Christianity
For where your treasure is, there will your heart be also.

(Matthew chapter 6 verse 21)

In my (Heavenly) Father's house are many mansions...I go to prepare a place for you.

(John chapter 14 verse 2)

Look not at the things which are seen (the earthly or material world), but at the things which are not seen (the spiritual realm): for the things which are seen are temporal; but the things which are not seen are eternal.

(2 Corinthians chapter 4 verse 18)

Confucianism
If you control the people by government acts and keep them in line with law and order, they will refrain from doing wrong, but they will not have a sense of honour or shame. But if you lead them through virtue and regulate them by the laws of propriety,

then they will have a sense of shame and will attain goodness.

(Analects)

The truth must be genuinely and earnestly realized by each person on their own.

(Chu Hsi on the Great Ultimate: Chu tzu ch'uan-shu)

Einstein

True religion is real living; living with all one's soul, with all one's goodness and righteousness.

(Albert Einstein)

Gandhi

God has no religion.

(Mohandas Gandhi)

Islam

God guides on the right path whom He wills.

(The Cattle chapter 6 verse 39)

(God's Commandments are) His right path, so follow it... This He has ordained for you that you may become pious.

(The Cattle chapter 6 verse 153)

Know that God steps in between a person and their heart.

(The Spoils chapter 8 verse 24)

It is not the eyes which are blind, but it is the hearts which are within the breasts which are blind.

(The Pilgrimage chapter 22 verse 46)

The servants of the Merciful God...shall be recompensed with a high place (heaven); for that they endured patiently.

(The Discrimination chapter 25 verse 75)

God has created the seven heavens one above another.

(The Kingdom chapter 67 verse 3)

God is the Lord of the ascents (the ways of ascent to the seven heavens).

(The Ways of Ascent chapter 70 verse 3)

Jainism

The spirits who are gifted with various virtues live one above the other (in ascending heavens), shining forth like the great luminaries and hoping never to descend (to earth) thence.

(Uttaradhyayana: Living Beings and the Round of Rebirth: Third Lecture: The Four Requisites)

The venerable ascetic Mahavira was...circumspect (cautious)...guarding his thoughts, guarding his words, guarding his acts, guarding his senses, guarding his chastity; without wrath, without pride, without deceit, without greed; calm, tranquil, composed, liberated, free from temptations, without egoism, without property; he had cut off all earthly ties and was not stained by any worldliness.

(Mahavira as Liberator: Kalpasutra)

Judaism

I have set before you life and death...therefore choose life.

(Deuteronomy chapter 30 verse 19)

Receive the (Divine) Law from God's mouth and lay up His words in your heart.

(Job chapter 22 verse 22)

Forget not God's Law; but let your heart keep God's commandments...Let not mercy and truth forsake you...write them upon the table of your heart.

(Proverbs chapter 3 verses 1 and 3)

Sikhism

Beyond this earth there are more worlds, more and more.

(The Repetition of the Divine Name: The Japji)

By hearing the Divine Name, the depth of the sea of virtue is sounded...By obeying God one forms an alliance with virtue.

(The Repetition of the Divine Name: The Japji)

Precious stones, jewels and gems shall be treasured up in your heart if you hearken to even one word of God.

(Guru Nanak's Japji)

God may bestow virtue on those who are devoid of it, as well as on those who already possess it.

(Guru Nanak's Japji)

Taoism

One offers incense and pronounces the vows, causing the heart to ascend to the heavens.

(The Teachings of Master Chuang)

The wise attend to the inner significance of things and do not concern themselves with outward appearances. Therefore they ignore matter (materialism and worldliness) and seek the spirit (spiritual treasures).

(Lao Tzu, Tao Te Ching (Avoiding Desire) chapter 12)

Spirit is reality. At its heart is truth.

(Lao Tzu, Tao Te Ching (The Heart of Emptiness) chapter 21)

They who do not esteem instruction or value their life, though they may be otherwise intelligent, become confused. Herein lies the significance of spirituality.

(Lao Tzu, Tao Te Ching (The Function of Skill) chapter 27)

Essential *teh* (virtue) makes no show (pretentious display) of itself, and therefore it is really virtuous. Inferior virtue never loses sight of itself and therefore it is no longer virtue.

(Lao Tzu, Tao Te Ching (A Discussion About *Teh* (Virtue)) chapter 38)

The great Tao (although it is difficult to define, the eternal and unchanging Way or the Universal Principle or Ultimate Pure Essence underlying all reality and existence/the spiritual force that pervades everything as well as spiritual discipline and bestower of all forms of life) is very plain, but people prefer the bypaths (an indirect course).

(Lao Tzu, Tao Te Ching (Gain by Insight) chapter 53)

The Tao is...the good person's treasure, the bad person's last resort.

(Lao Tzu, Tao Te Ching (The Practice of Tao) chapter 62)

Profound *teh* (virtue) is deep indeed...the very opposite of common things.

(Lao Tzu, Tao Te Ching (The *Teh* (Virtue) of Simplicity) chapter 65)

Zen Buddhism

More valuable than treasures in a storehouse are the treasures of the body. The most valuable of all are the treasures of the heart.

(Nichiren)

Zoroastrianism

Recollect that your body will return to dust, but your soul, if rich in good works, will mount to immortality...Take less care of your body and more of your soul; the pains and aches of the body are easily cured, but who can minister to the diseases of the soul?

(The Vision of Arda-Viraf)

Chapter 2

Absence of Anger and Bitterness

Anger is a strongly felt and disruptive emotion of displeasure aroused by real or perceived wrongs, or when the desire for what one considers to bring happiness and contentment or what one considers to be one's due is hindered and things do not turn out as one had hoped. Anger produces disequilibrium, foreseeable and consequential suffering and strife, challenges our peaceful and contented nature, and impedes our attempt to become closer to God.

Anger may be avoided by practicing the virtues of unconditional love, patience, restraint, forgiveness and detachment from worldly objects, pleasures and one's selfish desires and by surrender to God. One who is slow to wrath is of great understanding (Proverbs chapter 14 verse 29).

By reining in anger, one may escape strife and a lifetime of regret and sorrow.

Scriptural References

Buddhism

Do not wish harm to another out of anger or resentment.

(Sutta Nipata, Uragavagga, Mettasutta chapter 1.8.6 verse 147)

Those who hold back arisen anger like a whirling chariot, they I call a real charioteer; others only hold the reins.

(The Dhammapada chapter 17 (Anger) verse 222)

Overcome anger by love.

(The Dhammapada chapter 17 (Anger) verse 223)

Christianity

Whosoever is angry with another without a cause shall be in

danger of the judgment...Therefore if you bring your gift to the altar and there remember that another has ought [duty or obligation] against you; leave there your gift before the altar and go your way; first be reconciled to (that person) and then come and offer your gift.

(Matthew chapter 5 verses 22-24)

Let everyone be swift to hear, slow to speak and slow to wrath.

(James chapter 1 verse 19)

Let all bitterness and wrath and anger and clamour and evil speaking be put away from you, with all malice.

(Ephesians chapter 4 verse 31)

Confucianism

When anger arises, think of the consequences.

(Confucius)

Hinduism

Absence of anger.

(Saintly Virtue No. 12 of those endowed with a Divine Nature: Bhagavad-Gita chapter 16, verses 1-3)

Against an angry person do not in return show anger, bless when you are cursed.

(The Laws of Manu: Manava-dharma-sastra chapter 6 verses 33-60)

Islam

Those who...restrain their anger and pardon others...God loves.

(The Family of Imran chapter 3 verse 134)

Jainism

Wrath is a passion which defiles the soul.

(Sutrakrtanga (Praise of Mahavira) Book 1 Sixth Lecture)

An ascetic is free from anger.

(Sutrakrtanga (Carefulness) Book 1 Tenth Lecture)

Those who are of a wrathful disposition...do harm to themselves.

(Sutrakrtanga (The Real Truth) Book 1 Thirteenth Lecture)

Judaism

One who is slow to wrath is of great understanding.

(Proverbs chapter 14 verse 29)

A soft answer turns away wrath: but grievous words stir up anger.

(Proverbs chapter 15 verse 1)

One who is slow to anger appeases strife.

(Proverbs chapter 15 verse 18)

The discretion of a person defers anger.

(Proverbs chapter 19 verse 11)

Wrath brings forth strife.

(Proverbs chapter 30 verse 33)

Be not hasty in your spirit to be angry: for anger rests in the bosom of fools.

(Ecclesiastes chapter 7 verse 9)

The Lord is merciful and gracious, slow to anger and plenteous in mercy.

(Psalms chapter 103 verse 8)

Sikhism

Anger.

(One of five Sikh deadly sins)

O God, save us from the sin of wrath.

(The Community and its Past Saints: A Congregational Prayer)

Taoism

They who fight the best fight are not wrathful.

(Lao Tzu, Tao Te Ching (Compliance with Heaven) chapter 68)

Zoroastrianism

Indulge in no wrathfulness, for when one indulges in wrath they become forgetful of their duty and good works...and sin and crime of every kind occur unto their mind.

(Commandments for the Body and the Soul)

Be not wrathful-minded.

(Admonitions)

Chapter 3

Absence of Covetousness, Greed and Envy

Greed and covetousness involve an inordinate or rapacious desire to possess things such as material wealth, fame and glory and to experience gratification of the senses, all of which are transient and illusory. On a more basic level, they manifest in a desire to accumulate more than what one legitimately needs to maintain the body. This desire to relentlessly acquire wealth and possessions, personal fame and recognition continues against a backdrop of suppression of appreciation that all must be left behind upon death. Envy involves a discontented or restless feeling arising from witnessing another's perceived success or material advantage.

Release from the bonds of avarice, greed and envy through greater self-control and non-possessiveness or non-attachment will lead to inner peace and contentment. Rest content and be thankful for what one has been blessed and gifted with by God. It is better rather to crave spiritual treasures of the heart.

Therefore lay up for yourselves treasures in Heaven (Matthew chapter 6 verse 20). This worldly life is no more than a temporary illusion (Qur'an (Iron) chapter 57 verse 20).

When you reduce yourself to nothing and are contented thereby, you have everything.

Scriptural References

Baha'i
Free from envy, enter the presence of Unity.
(Of Disputation and Fault-Finding: Words of Wisdom from the Supreme Pen of Baha'u'llah)

Buddhism

Riches make most people greedy. Any possession that increases the sin of selfishness...is nothing but a drawback in disguise.

(Jatakamala chapter 5 verses 5 and 15)

"These children and riches are mine"; thinking thus the fool is troubled. Since no one even owns oneself, what is the sense in "my children and riches"? Verily, it is the law of humanity that though one accumulates hundreds of thousands of worldly goods, one still succumbs to the spell of death.

(Udanavarga chapter 1 verses 20-1)

The wise do not befriend the avaricious (those with an insatiable greed for riches).

(Udanavarga chapter 25 verse 1)

The uncharitable do not go to the world of the gods.

(The Dhammapada chapter 13 (The World) verse 177)

Take care that greediness and vice do not bring you to grief.

(The Dhammapada chapter 18 (Impurity) verse 248)

One should not despise what one receives and one should not envy the gain of others.

(The Dhammapada chapter 25 (The Bhikshu/Mendicant) verse 365)

Christianity

Take heed and beware of covetousness; for a person's life (richness of the soul) consists not in the abundance of (worldly) things which are possessed.

(Luke chapter 12 verse 15)

Do not lay up for yourselves treasures upon earth, where moth and rust corrupt and where thieves break through and steal. But lay up for yourselves treasures in heaven, where neither moth nor rust corrupt and where thieves do not break through nor steal. For where your treasure is, there will your heart be also.

(Matthew chapter 6 verses 19-21)

Be without covetousness and be content with such things as you have.

(Hebrews chapter 13 verse 5)

Hinduism
Absence of covetousness.

(Saintly Virtue No. 17 of those endowed with a Divine Nature: Bhagavad-Gita chapter 16, verses 1-3)

Islam
Humanity covets...gold and silver. This is the pleasure of the present world's life, but God has the excellent return (Paradise) with Him.

(The Family of Imran chapter 3 verse 14)

Never let those who covetously withhold the wealth which God has bestowed on them out of His bounty think it is good for them: indeed it is an evil thing for them.

(The Family of Imran chapter 3 verse 180)

Do not covet the things in which God has made some of you to excel over others.

(The Women chapter 4 verse 32)

Souls are prone to greed. But if you act kindly and fear God... know that God is aware of all your actions.

(The Women chapter 4 verse 128)

Strain not your eyes enviously at which We have bestowed on others to enjoy.

(The Rock chapter 15 verse 88)

Know that this worldly life is but a sport and play and adornment...and hoarding of money...This worldly life (is no more than a temporary illusion).

(Iron chapter 57 verse 20)

Those who are saved from their own covetousness, they are the prosperous (spiritually enlightened).

(Cheating chapter 64 verse 16)

I seek refuge in the Lord...from the evil of the envious.

(The Daybreak chapter 113 verses 1-5)

Jainism

Greed is a passion which defiles the soul.

(Sutrakrtanga (Praise of Mahavira) Book 1 Sixth Lecture)

Forgetting that life will have an end, the rash and foolish are full of selfishness; they toil day and night, greedy of wealth, as if they never grow old or die.

(Sutrakrtanga (Carefulness) Book 1 Tenth Lecture)

Judaism

You shall not covet your neighbour's house, you shall not covet your neighbour's wife, nor manservant, nor maidservant, nor ox, nor ass, nor anything that is your neighbour's.

(The Ten Commandments: Commandment No. 10 Exodus chapter 20 verse 17)

Let not your heart envy sinners.

(Proverbs chapter 23 verse 17)

Wrath is cruel and anger is outrageous; but who is able to stand before envy?

(Proverbs chapter 27 verse 4)

Sikhism

Covetousness.

(One of five Sikh deadly sins)

O God, save us from the sin of greed.

(The Community and its Past Saints: A Congregational Prayer)

Taoism

(Those who seek immortality) must not envy those superior to them.

(The Reward for Deeds: p'ao-p'u Tzu)

Zoroastrianism

Be not covetous...Cherish not wicked envy.

(Admonitions)

Avarice and ambition...will plunge (humanity) into everlasting misery.

(The Vision of Arda-Viraf)

Bear no improper envy, so that your life may not become meaningless.

(Commandments for the Body and the Soul)

Form no covetous desire, so that the demon of greediness may not deceive thee...With a greedy person you should not be a partner.

(Commandments for the Body and the Soul)

Chapter 4

Absence of Enmity, Hatred and a Desire for Revenge

Hatred involves an intense dislike or detestation of the person or object at which this negative emotion is directed. Enmity encompasses feelings of hatred, hostility, ill-will, antagonism and animosity. These emotions are often accompanied by a thirst for revenge or retaliation for actual or perceived wrongs or injuries, inevitably leading to strife and consequential bloodshed and destruction. The Law of Attraction is such that hatred begets hatred in turn. Therefore, one should respond to hatred with kindness (Lao Tzu).

Such strong, controlling and consuming emotions defile the soul and must be overcome by developing a circuit-breaker: peaceful and positive feelings of love, empathy and compassion towards their objects, as well as acknowledgment that a portion of God's spirit resides in us all. Neither should grudges be carried nor retaliatory acts undertaken; only good thoughts and deeds, patient understanding and forgiveness should follow.

One must let go and free oneself of such corrosive and consuming feelings if one wishes to be healed and whole again.

Scriptural References

Baha'i

Purge thy mind of malice and...enter the presence of Unity.

(Of Disputation and Fault-Finding: Words of Wisdom from the Supreme Pen of Baha'u'llah)

Buddhism

"They abused me, they beat me, they defeated me, they robbed me": the hatred of those who harbor such thoughts will never cease.

(The Dhammapada chapter 1 (The Twin-Verses) verse 3)

Hatred does not cease in this world by hatred: hatred ceases by love; this is an eternal truth.

(The Dhammapada chapter 1 (The Twin-Verses) verse 5)

Let us live happily then, not hating those who hate us! Among those who hate us let us dwell free from hatred!

(The Dhammapada chapter 15 (Happiness) verse 197)

There is no shark (grip) like hatred.

(The Dhammapada chapter 18 (Impurity) verse 251)

Christianity

Love your enemies, bless them who curse you, do good to them who hate you and pray for them who despitefully (maliciously) use you and persecute you. That you may be children of your Father...in Heaven: for He makes His sun to rise on the evil and on the good and sends rain on the just and on the unjust.

(Matthew chapter 5 verses 44-5)

Love your enemies, do good to those who hate you.

(Luke chapter 6 verse 27)

Hinduism

By the restraint of (one's) senses, by the destruction of...hatred and by the abstention from injuring...creatures, (one) becomes fit for immortality.

(The Laws of Manu: Manava-dharma-sastra chapter 6 verses 33-60)

Bearing enmity towards none.

(Saintly Virtue No. 25 of those endowed with a Divine Nature: Bhagavad-Gita chapter 16 verses 1-3)

Islam

The servants of the Merciful God are those who walk upon the earth in humility and when the ignorant (rude and aggressive) address them, say 'Peace!'.

(The Discrimination chapter 25 verse 63)

Judaism

You shall not hate your neighbor in your heart...You shall not avenge, nor bear any grudge...but you shall love your neighbor as yourself: I am the Lord.

(Leviticus chapter 19 verses 17-18)

Hatred stirs up strife: but love covers all sins.

(Proverbs chapter 10 verse 12)

Say not, I will do to them as they have done to me: I will render to the person according to their work (deeds).

(Proverbs chapter 24 verse 29)

Taoism

One should respond to hatred with kindness.

(Lao Tzu, Tao Te Ching (A Consideration of Beginnings) chapter 63)

Chapter 5

Absence of Stealing

Stealing is the taking of something dishonestly or wrongfully or appropriating something to oneself without right or acknowledgment. It is considered so morally reprehensible that it is prohibited by the *Ten Commandments* and is criminalized in the secular and religious law of virtually every country. It is considered a defilement of the soul, as it harms and violates not only the victims but the perpetrator as well.

The Divine proscription against stealing is to encourage us to let go of our cravings, greed, covetousness, our desire for fame and glory, possessiveness and attachment and to avoid exploiting others for one's advantage. Basically, we are called upon not to take what is not freely given to us nor cause others to steal on our behalf (and also not to conduct ourselves in such a manner as to foreseeably tempt others to steal from us). One should also not steal or rob from oneself.

Scriptural References

Buddhism
Avoid taking anything that is not freely given.

(Second Basic Precept or Virtue)

Do not appropriate to oneself what is not given by stealing or theft.

(The Five Precepts and their Meaning: Buddhagosa's Commentary: Papanasudani)

Abstain from taking what is not given.

(Khuddakapatha 2)

Stealing is defilement.

(Sutta Nipata, Kulavagga, Amagandhasutta, chapter 2.2.4

verse 242)

Christianity
For out of the heart proceed...thefts...These are the things which defile a person.

(Matthew chapter 15 verses 19-20)

Islam
They who cheat shall on the Day of Resurrection bring with them that which they have stolen. Then shall each soul be paid what it has earned.

(The Family of Imran chapter 3 verse 161)

Do not approach the property of the orphan except to improve it, until the orphan is of (mature) age...And give full measure when you measure and weigh with a right (accurate) balance; that is better and fairer.

(The Journey by Night chapter 17 verses 34-5)

Jainism
I renounce all taking of anything not given...I shall neither take myself what is not given, nor cause others to take it, nor consent to their taking it.

(Third Great Vow: Acaranga Sutra)

Judaism
You shall not steal.

(The Ten Commandments: Commandment No. 8 Exodus chapter 20 verse 15)

Taoism
Not prizing rare treasures deters (one) from becoming a thief.

(Lao Tzu, Tao Te Ching (Quieting People) chapter 3)

The wise wear wool (rather than silk) and keep their gems out of sight.

(Lao Tzu, Tao Te Ching (The Difficulty of Understanding) chapter 70)

Zoroastrianism

Rob not the property of others.

(Admonitions)

Chapter 6

Austerity

Austerity may be variously defined as a lack of luxury or ornament or, at the extreme, the pursuit of a severe or ascetic practice, involving self-denial (such as fasting) and restraint of the senses. On a spiritual level, austerity involves the voluntary acceptance of varying levels of hardships for purification of the body, mind and spirit, and for the removal of pain, suffering and anxiety. One's inherent pleasure-seeking senses are thereby restrained and disciplined. The consumption of only that which is really necessary to sustain life and the renunciation of sensual pleasures are designed to rectify and atone for breaches of spiritual tenets and so to more closely align the soul to God. Indeed, instances of self-denial may be offered up to God in love and worship.

At its core, austerity involves self-mastery of the senses and the elimination of life's nonessentials to the greatest extent practicable (varying, of necessity, as between individuals) so that distractions fall away and a stronger focus may be maintained on the eternal truths and the other Divine Virtues. Those who make themselves poor have great riches (Proverbs chapter 13 verse 7).

Scriptural References

Buddhism
If by leaving a small treasure one sees a great treasure, let a wise person leave the small treasure and look to the great. (The wise one leaves aside limited pleasures, looking to far-reaching happiness.)

(The Dhammapada Chapter 21 (Miscellaneous) verse 290)

Christianity
Blessed are the poor in spirit: for theirs is the Kingdom of Heaven.

(Matthew chapter 5 verse 3)

It is easier for a camel to go through a needle's eye, than for a rich man to enter the Kingdom of God.

(Luke chapter 18 verse 25)

Confucianism
With rough rice to eat and water to drink and one's bent arm to be a pillow, there is still contentment.

(Confucius' Conversation and Manners: Analects)

Hinduism
Let one accept so much only as will sustain life.

(The Laws of Manu: Manava-dharma-sastra chapter 6 verses 33-60)

Austerity.

(Saintly Virtue No. 8 of those endowed with a Divine Nature: Bhagavad-Gita chapter 16 verses 1-3)

Islam
Believers, fasting is prescribed for you as it was prescribed for those before you (so that you may be mindful of God).

(The Cow chapter 2 verse 183)

The servants of the Merciful God are those who walk upon the earth lowly (modestly/humbly).

(The Discrimination chapter 25 verse 63)

Jainism
Practise austerities for the removal of pain.

(Sutrakrtanga (Praise of Mahavira) Book 1 Sixth Lecture)

Chastity is the highest of austerities.

(Sutrakrtanga (Praise of Mahavira) Book 1 Sixth Lecture)

A monk should be content with such food and drink as will sustain life.

(Sutrakrtanga (The Law) Book 1 Ninth Lecture)

A monk, who vigorously practises austerities, avoids anger and pride.

(Sutrakrtanga (The Path) Book 1 Eleventh Lecture)

As a large tank, when its supply of water has been stopped, dries up by the consumption of water and by evaporation, so the bad Karma of a monk, which they have acquired in millions of births, is annihilated by austerities.

(Uttaradhyayana (The Road of Penance) Thirtieth Lecture)

Judaism

Those who make themselves poor (by practising austerities) have great riches (treasures of the heart).

(Proverbs chapter 13 verse 7)

Chapter 7

Belief in One God (Monotheism/the Oneness of God)

There are many religious pathways to, but only, the one God to whom alone prayer and worship should be directed. There is only one Truth, not many. Truth is not the monopoly of any particular religion or individual, and attaching other labels to it demeans it. No particular religion or creed can lay claim to being the sole or exclusive interpreter or arbiter of the Truth.

This virtue entails obedience to, trust in, and worship of, only one eternal God, the Creator of all life and all that exists. God can never be described completely or comprehensively in words, because human language is too impoverished to express the essence or true nature of God. Although the Holy Scriptures of the mainstream religions have observed that God cannot be fully or completely comprehended or described in finite human terms or words (ineffable), they have identified at least the following Divine or supra-human qualities or attributes which are referenced in the scriptural passages which follow:

- God is the Creator and Sustainer of all life and all that exists, including the phenomenal world (Nature) in all of its diversity, and the absolute foundation of all things (including humanity, the spiritual realms, flora and fauna)
- God is Truth, the Word, the Light, Absolute Holiness and the Universal Divine Principle or Ultimate Reality
- God is a universal energy permeating or running through all things
- God is Love, Kindness and Tenderness
- God is Compassion and is All-Merciful and All-Forgiving

29

- God is immortal and eternal; without beginning and without end
- God is self-existent and self-subsistent (existing in and for Himself alone)
- God is incorporeal (a spiritual or nonmaterial/formless being)
- God is infinite (immeasurably great, unlimited, endless and innumerable)
- God is the transcendent Supreme Being
- God is immanent (His continuing presence or Divine spark of Love is indwelling or within each individual and connects all that is)
- God is unchanging
- God is All-Seeing
- God is omnipresent (present everywhere and in all things at the same time/there is no place that God is not)
- God is All-Mighty and All-Powerful/omnipotent (having infinite and unlimited power and authority)
- God is All-Wise and omniscient (knowing all things and having infinite knowledge of everything that has passed and everything that will be/nothing is, or can be, hidden from God)
- God is a benevolent provider (His providential care, protection and guardianship extend to all living sentient beings)

Ponder the following mysteries and miracles. Does time have a beginning and an end? Is time always linear or is it nonlinear? Does space have a beginning and an end? What is the highest number? How many universes exist? How many life forms exist? How many spiritual realms and dimensions exist? What makes the human heart beat? And the computer that is the human brain? Consider the spectrum of colors of the rainbow, the splendor and interdependence of the natural world and the miracle of life. And the nonrandomized nature of the operation of the physical laws of the universe, increasing scientific research into the post-death phenomenon of continuing consciousness and the reconciliation and convergence of God and science with recent discoveries in subatomic quantum physics.

When one tries to grasp these metaphysical questions and contemplations, one is left with a feeling of humility and utter inadequacy and futility concerning the finiteness of human comprehension in describing the Lord of Infinity and His Domain. One can only feel a sense of wonder and reverential awe.

Scriptural References

Baha'i

My (God's) Eternity is My creation. I have created it for you. My Oneness is My design. I have designed it for you; therefore clothe yourself with it...O Dead Men...you are drowned in the sea of polytheism while talking of Oneness. Oneness, in its true significance, means that God alone should be realized as the One Power which animates and dominates all things, which are but manifestations of its energy.

(Of Oneness: Words of Wisdom from the Supreme Pen of Baha'u'llah)

I have placed in you the essence of My Light. Therefore be illumined by it and seek no one else but Me.

(Of the Light: Words of Wisdom from the Supreme Pen of Baha'u'llah)

The Word is the Fire of God which, glowing in the hearts of people, burns away all things that are not of God.

(Of the Light: Words of Wisdom from the Supreme Pen of Baha'u'llah)

Turn from all save Me; for My Authority is eternal...My Kingdom is lasting and shall not be overthrown. If you seek another than Me...your search shall be in vain.

(Of Divine Humanity: Words of Wisdom from the Supreme Pen of Baha'u'llah)

Christianity

In the beginning was the Word, and the Word was with God and the Word was God...All things were made by Him; and without Him was not any thing made that was made.

(John chapter 1 verses 1 and 3)

God is a spirit: and they who worship Him must worship Him in spirit and in truth (obeying His commandments).

(John chapter 4 verse 24)

The Kingdom of God is within you (the Divine attribute of immanence).

(Luke chapter 17 verse 21)

God is love.

(1 John chapter 4 verse 8)

Confucianism

Sacrifices to Heaven and earth are meant for the service of the Lord on High.

(The Reverence for Ancestors: Doctrine of the Mean)

There is only one Great Ultimate, yet each of the myriad things has been endowed with it and each in itself possesses the Great Ultimate...which is not spatially conditioned; it has neither corporeal form nor body (the Divine attributes of immanence and omnipresence).

(Chu Hsi on the Great Ultimate: Chu tzu ch'uan-shu)

Gandhi

There is no other God than Truth.

(Mohandas Gandhi, *An Autobiography*)

Hinduism

The Great Soul...exercises universal overlordship...One God... is the source of all...Him Who is...'incorporeal'.

(The One God and the Phenomenal World: Svetasvatara Upanisad)

My (God's) shape is unmanifest, but I pervade the world.

(Everything is a Sacrifice to Me: Bhagavad-Gita chapter 9)

You (the Lord) are the...absolute foundation of all things.

(The Absolute Foundation of All Things: Bhagavad-Gita)

I (the Lord) am omnipresent as the stormwind which resides in space.

(Everything is a Sacrifice to Me: Bhagavad-Gita chapter 9)

Islam

There is no God save Allah.

(The Kalima or Creed of Islam)

God is the Inner, who is immanent in all things.

(The Heights (or The Wall with Elevations) chapter 7 verse 180; Muhammad al-Madani The Ninety-Nine Most Beautiful Names of Allah (No. 9))

God is the Truth.

(The Heights (or The Wall with Elevations) chapter 7 verse 180; Muhammad al-Madani The Ninety-Nine Most Beautiful Names of Allah (No. 18))

Your God is one God. There is no god but He, the Merciful, the Compassionate.

(The Cow chapter 2 verse 163)

Allah is the patron (protector or guardian) of those who believe. He brings them forth from darkness into light.

(The Cow chapter 2 verse 257)

Truly, there is nothing hidden from God in the earth, nor in the heaven...There is no god but He, the Mighty, the Wise.

(The Family of Imran Chapter 3 verses 5-6)

Not a leaf falls, but God knows it.

(The Cattle chapter 6 verse 59)

God's Word is the Truth.

(The Cattle chapter 6 verse 73)

No vision can see Him (God), but He perceives all vision.

(The Cattle chapter 6 verse 103)

God knows the seen (material realms) and the unseen (spiritual realms).

(The Repentance chapter 9 verse 105)

God has power over all things.

((Prophet) Hud chapter 11 verse 4)

God is the Word of Truth.

(The Thunder chapter 13 verse 14)

God is the Creator of all things.

(The Thunder chapter 13 verse 16)

Verily, your Lord is the All-Knowing Creator.

(The Rock chapter 15 verse 88)

Do not make up images or comparisons for God (as there is nothing similar to Him).

(The Bee chapter 16 verse 74)

Set not up with God other gods, or you will sit despised and forsaken. Your Lord has decreed you shall not serve any other than Him.

(The Journey by Night chapter 17 verse 22)

God alone is the Truth (having no partners or rivals).

(The Pilgrimage chapter 22 verse 62)

God has knowledge of everything done by those who are in the heavens and the earth (the Divine attribute of omniscience).

(The Light chapter 24 verse 41)

Sufficient is your Lord as a good Guide and Helper.

(The Discrimination chapter 25 verse 31)

The servants of the Merciful God are those...who call not upon another god with God (those who never invoke any other deity).

(The Discrimination chapter 25 verse 68)

He is God; there is no God but He *La ilaha illa Huwa* (none has the right to be worshipped but He), to Him belongs all praise in the first (this world) and in the last (the Hereafter)...to Him shall you (your soul) be returned.

(The Story chapter 28 verse 70)

God's is the highest description in the heavens and in the earth (there is nothing comparable to Him).

(The Romans/Greeks/Byzantines chapter 30 verse 27)

God is the Creator of the heavens and the earth...There is nothing like Him, for He both hears and sees all.

(The Counsel chapter 42 verse 11)

God knows what the soul whispers and God is nearer than the jugular vein (immanence).

(Qaf chapter 50 verse 16)

God is the First (nothing is before Him) and the Last (nothing is after Him), the Most High (nothing is above Him) and the Most Near (nothing is nearer than Him). And He knows all things.

(Iron chapter 57 verse 3)

God is the One and only God, the Eternal God. He begets none, and is not begotten. None is equal to Him.

(Unity chapter 112 verses 1-4)

Jainism

The transcendent; its essence is without form (incorporeal).

(Acaranga Sutra: First Book Fifth Lecture Sixth Lesson Essence of the World: The Consciousness of Liberation)

Judaism

Hear O Israel: The Lord our God is One Lord. And you shall love the Lord your God with all your heart and with all your soul and with all your might. And these words...shall be in your heart.

(Deuteronomy chapter 6 verses 4-6)

You shall have no other gods before Me.

(The Ten Commandments: Commandment No. 1 Exodus chapter 20 verse 3)

The Lord is good; for His mercy, tender kindness and steadfast love endure forever.

(Jeremiah chapter 33 verse 11)

You are a God of forgiveness. Gracious and compassionate. Slow to anger and abounding in loving-kindness.

(Nehemiah chapter 9 verse 17)

The Lord...is merciful and gracious, slow to anger and plenteous in mercy and loving-kindness.

(Psalms chapter 103 verse 8)

In wisdom have You made them all; the earth is full of your creatures...These all look to You to give them food in due season...when You open Your hand, they are filled with good things (benevolent provider).

(Psalms chapter 104 verses 24, 27-8)

The eyes of the Lord are in every place (the Divine attributes of omnipresence/omniscience).

(Proverbs chapter 15 verse 3)

Pygmy

In the beginning was God, today is God, tomorrow will be God. Who can make an image of God? He has no body. He is as a word.

(A Traditional Pygmy Hymn on God)

Shintoism

God is not a terrible (vengeful) being, but One that extends divine help and is fondly esteemed and toward whom gratitude is felt. And the relationship between God and (humanity) is extremely intimate.

(A Coalescent Harmony between Humankind and Nature: Kokutai no Hongi)

Sikhism

There is one God. He is the supreme truth. He, the Creator, is without fear and without hate. He, the Omnipresent, pervades the universe. He is not born, nor does He die to be born again. By His grace shall thou worship Him. Before time itself there was truth. When time began to run its course He was the truth. Even now, He is the truth and evermore shall truth prevail.

(Mul Mantra)

There is but one God whose name is true, the Creator, devoid of fear and enmity, immortal, unborn, self-existent, great and beneficent. The True One was in the beginning...The True One is now also...The True One also shall be. By thinking I cannot obtain a conception of Him.

(God as Truth: Guru Nanak's Japji)

God is not established, nor is He created. The pure one exists by Himself.

(God as Truth: Guru Nanak's Japji)

Who can sing Him, Who appears to be far, but is known to be near (immanence)? Who can sing Him, Who is all-seeing and omnipresent? In describing Him there would be never an end. Millions of men give millions upon millions of descriptions of Him, but they fail to describe Him.

(God as Truth: Guru Nanak's Japji)

God is everywhere contained (omnipresence)...He cannot be described by words...There is but one Bestower on all living beings.

(God as Truth: Guru Nanak's Japji)

Thou (referring to God), O Formless One (incorporeal/of spirit).

(The Repetition of the Divine Name: The Japji)

The Lord...gives life to all the world, His light shines in all life born.

(Spiritual Marriage: The Bara Mah)

The light which is in everything is Thine, O Lord of Light.

(From the Sohila: Guru Nanak)

Thou, O God, the one Supreme Being, are fully contained in every heart and pervade everything (the Divine attributes of immanence and omnipresence).

(From the Rahiras: Guru Ram Das)

God is the pure Being...O God, Thou art the true Creator. All creatures are thine; You provide for them all...You are the totally infinite Supreme Being...You are the same in every age... You are the eternal Creator.

(From the Rahiras: Guru Ram Das)

The One God is in every place...He is in the soul and the soul is in Him.

(Hymn by Guru Arjan)

Taoism

The Tao (Way or the eternal and unchanging spirit or energy which permeates all life and matter) is unseen, empty, yet also profound and the creator of all that is.

(Lao Tzu, Tao Te Ching (The Meaning of Taoist Emptiness) chapter 4)

It is unseen because it is colorless; it is unheard because it is soundless; when seeking to grasp it, it eludes one, because it is incorporeal...It is called the transcendental.

(Lao Tzu, Tao Te Ching (In Praise of the Profound) chapter 14)

(Referring to the Tao or Way) There is Being that is all-inclusive and that existed before Heaven and Earth. Calm, indeed, and incorporeal! It is alone and changeless. Everywhere it functions unhindered...I do not know its nature; if I try to characterize it, I will call it Tao (the Way).

(Lao Tzu, Tao Te Ching (Describing the Mysterious) chapter 25)

The Ten (Native American) Indian Commandments

Remain close to the Great Spirit (Wakan Tanka: Lakota Tribe).

(Commandment No. 2)

Zoroastrianism

If you...understand the commandments which the Wise One (Ahura Mazda (God)) has given, well-being...and salvation for the righteous...shall hereafter be for the best.

(The Primordial Choice: Gatha: Yasna 30)

Ahura-Mazda (God), Heavenly, Holiest, Creator of the corporeal (material) world, Peace!

(The Soul's Destination)

Chapter 8

Charity and Service

Charity is the noble expression of the benevolence of the mighty (The Buddha). To adapt from the old proverb, charity is putting our money and possessions where our mouth is. Charity is giving freely of what one has to the needy without expecting anything in return.

Charity may be variously defined as almsgiving, benevolence and the relief of needy or unfortunate persons or outcasts in distress by giving away one's possessions or through acts of service. It also encompasses a civic duty or responsibility aspect; using God-given skills, talents and abilities for the service and betterment of one's immediate community and wider society. Although charity is most commonly associated with material charity which is done primarily for the welfare of the body (such as food, clothing and shelter) and which assists others temporarily, spiritual charity assists the soul by ending separation from God, the cause of suffering.

The attitude underlying the act of charity is as important for the soul as the act of charity itself. It should never be undertaken grudgingly. One should selflessly and unconditionally share, quietly (indeed privately and secretly) and without fanfare and ostentation, what one possesses (and even cherishes) instinctively as the right thing to do, without any expectation of earthly reward or benefit, praise or fame. Charity should never be withheld from one who asks, regardless of how we perceive the genuineness of the request or the motive behind it. It is our intention and good faith that really matter.

Charity should also be undertaken totally for the love of God and God's needy with a sense of appreciation to God for the means and opportunity to assist others who are needy and vulnerable. From an Islamic context, one is making a 'loan' to God. The Divine Law of Giving is such that whatever charity one renders to others will be returned to the giver many times over in the form of God's abundant blessings (heavenly or spiritual treasures). God will repay the loan with abundant interest!

Charity is the knowledge of eternity that is God (Sikh scripture).

Scriptural References

Baha'i
Charity is beloved and acceptable before God and is accounted the chief among all good deeds.

(Tablet of Baha'u'llah: Words of Paradise)

The effect of deeds is in truth more powerful than that of words.

(Of the Light: Words of Wisdom from the Supreme Pen of Baha'u'llah)

Buddhism
Giving is the noble expression of the benevolence of the mighty. Even dust, given in childhood innocence, is a good gift. No gift that is given in good faith to a worthy recipient can be called small; its effect is so great.

(Jatakamala chapter 3 verse 23)

The wise one...rejoicing in charity becomes thereby blessed in the beyond.

(The Dhammapada chapter 13 (The World) verse 177)

If you light a lamp for another, it will also brighten your own path.

(Buddhist proverb)

Christianity
Give to those who ask of you and from those who would borrow

from you, do not turn away.

(Matthew chapter 5 verse 42)

When you give alms, let not your left hand know what your right hand is doing. Give your alms in secret: and your Father (in Heaven) Who sees in secret shall reward you openly.

(Matthew chapter 6 verses 3-4)

If you wish to be perfect, sell your possessions and give the money to the poor and you will have treasure in heaven.

(Matthew chapter 19 verse 21)

The Son of Man (Jesus Christ) came not to be served but to serve.

(Mark chapter 10 verse 45)

Give and it shall be given unto you; good measure, pressed down and shaken together and running over, shall they give into your bosom. For with the same measure that you use, it shall be measured to you again.

(Luke chapter 6 verse 38)

My prayers and gifts to the poor have come up as a memorial offering before God.

(Acts chapter 10 verse 4)

Those who sow sparingly shall reap also sparingly; and those who sow bountifully shall reap also bountifully. Every one according as they purpose in their heart, so let them give; not grudgingly, or of necessity: for God loves a cheerful giver.

(2 Corinthians chapter 9 verses 6-7)

Be doers of the Word (the Divine Message, the Truth or Law), and not hearers only...Whoso looks into the perfect law of liberty and continues therein, being not a forgetful hearer, but a doer of the Word, this person shall be blessed.

(James chapter 1 verses 22 and 25)

Confucianism

When the Great Tao (the Way) prevailed...helpless widows, orphans and cripples were well cared for. People...used their energies not for their own benefit.

(The Mythic Past: Li Chi (Classic of Ritual) Liyun)

Hinduism

Charity.

(Saintly Virtue No. 4 of those endowed with a Divine Nature: Bhagavad-Gita chapter 16 verses 1-3)

Giving (*datta*) constitutes one of the three cardinal virtues of Hinduism.

(The Three Da's: Brhadaranyaka Upanisad)

Islam

Righteousness is this...to give of one's wealth for the love of God to kinsmen and orphans, the poor, the traveller, beggars and to those in captivity.

(The Cow chapter 2 verse 177)

They (believers) ask you (Prophet Muhammad) what they should give in alms. Say: "The surplus." (what you can spare or that which is over and above your needs).

(The Cow chapter 2 verse 219)

Do not spoil your almsgiving...like those who spend their wealth for the sake of ostentation and do not believe in God... They shall gain nothing from their charitable works.

(The Cow chapter 2 verse 264)

To be charitable openly is good, but to give alms to the poor in private is better and will expiate for you your sins. God has knowledge of all your actions.

(The Cow chapter 2 verse 271)

Whatever alms you give shall benefit your soul, provided that you give them for the love of God. And whatever alms you give shall be repaid to you in full.

(The Cow chapter 2 verse 272)

Whatever alms you give are known to God. Those who give alms by day and night, in private and in public, shall be rewarded by their Lord. They shall have nothing to fear or to regret.

(The Cow chapter 2 verses 273-4)

You cannot attain to righteousness (piety) until you give in alms what you dearly cherish. The alms you give are known to God.

(The Family of Imran chapter 3 verse 92)

God does not love those...who are...miserly and enjoin others to be miserly; who hide the riches which God of His bounty has bestowed upon them.

(The Women chapter 4 verse 37)

Those who do good deeds shall be repaid many times over. God is forgiving and grateful (bountiful in His rewards).

(The Counsel chapter 42 verse 26)

Verily, those who give in charity...and lend God a goodly loan, it shall be doubled (to their credit) and theirs shall be a generous reward (Paradise).

(Iron chapter 57 verse 18)

God does not love those who are niggardly and enjoin upon others miserliness.

(Iron chapter 57 verse 24)

Jainism

Give up your wealth.

(The Simile of the Leaf: Uttaradhyayana)

Judaism

There are those who divest themselves (provide alms) for others and yet increase (in treasures of the heart): and there are those who withhold (from their possessions) more than is meet (appropriate), but it tends to poverty (of the heart).

(Proverbs chapter 11 verse 24)

Happy are those who are kind to the poor (the needy).

(Proverbs chapter 14 verse 21)

Those who have pity upon the poor (draw closer to) the

Lord: and what has been given will be repaid.

(Proverbs chapter 19 verse 17)

Those who shut their ears at the cry of the poor, they shall also cry themselves, but shall not be heard.

(Proverbs chapter 21 verse 13)

Those who have a bountiful eye shall be blessed; for they give of their bread to the poor.

(Proverbs chapter 22 verse 9)

Those who give unto the poor shall not lack.

(Proverbs chapter 28 verse 27)

When I bring all the tithes into the storehouse, that there may be food in God's house, the Lord of hosts will open the windows of Heaven for me and pour out such a blessing that there won't be room enough to receive it.

(Malachi chapter 3 verse 10)

Shintoism

Extend your benevolence to all...advance public good and promote common interests.

(The Japanese Ethos: Imperial Rescript on Education 30 October 1890 (modernized Shinto))

Sikhism

Give in charity (*dan*).

(Nanak's Call: A Janamsakhi)

Charity, almsgiving and prayer are the knowledge of eternity that is the Lord.

(Spiritual Marriage: The Bara Mah)

They alone are truly truthful (righteous) who give something in alms and in charity.

(Truth as the Heart of Conduct)

Taoism

Those who seek immortality must...relieve the destitute and

save the poor.

(The Reward for Deeds: p'ao-p'u Tzu)

Having given to others freely, (the wise person) will have in plenty (those who are generous and charitable towards others will be rewarded with abundant blessings and security).

(Lao Tzu, Tao Te Ching (The Nature of the Essential) chapter 81)

The Ten (Native American) Indian Commandments

Give assistance and kindness wherever needed.

(Commandment No. 5)

Zen Buddhism

That which you give to another will become your own sustenance; if you light a lamp for another, your own way will be lit.

(Nichiren)

Zoroastrianism

Do good works with good activity.

(Admonitions)

The will of the Lord is the Law of holiness. (Spiritual riches) shall be given to those who work in this world for Ahura-Mazda (God) and wield according to the will of Ahura the power He gave to them to relieve the poor.

(Prayer of Ahuna Vairya)

Chapter 9

Compassion (Humanity)

To seek God is to manifest compassion. Compassion is a feeling of tenderness, sorrow or pity for the sufferings, afflictions, distress or misfortunes of another. It comprises identification with, and understanding of, the plight of those who suffer and a natural and heartfelt desire to share and alleviate that suffering. The Abrahamic religions (Judaism, Christianity and Islam) as well as Taoism and Shintoism encourage believers to particularly bestow filial compassion and humanity on one's parents. Compassion is to be bestowed upon all living/sentient beings (including oneself) by transcending our natural propensity towards self-preoccupation and developing empathy (mindful entering into the feelings or spirit of another) and deep sympathy or pathos for their suffering. We weep for those who weep but we also rejoice and have joy in others' success, good fortune and happiness (the Buddhist concept of *mudita*). Therefore include others' happiness in your own joy (Paramahansa Yogananda).

While compassion includes both empathy and sympathy, it extends beyond them. The purest form of compassion comprises a natural and instinctive predisposition towards the well-being of sentient beings without any expectation of personal acknowledgment or reward. The Buddhist concept of *karuna* asks us to be a completely non-dualistic one with each suffering, troubled and afflicted living being we encounter by manifesting unconditional and boundless love towards them and their suffering, even to (or perhaps especially to) those who are not favorably disposed towards us. Compassion embraces qualities of the heart including love, charity and kindness. Until the last creature draws its final breath, we must show compassion.

Scriptural References

Baha'i

Under all circumstances, whether in adversity or comfort, in glory or affliction...show forth love and affection, compassion and union (unity).

(Tablet of Baha'u'llah)

Buddhism

As a mother would protect her only child at the risk of her own life, so let everyone cultivate a boundless mind towards all beings. Cultivate thoughts of boundless goodwill towards the whole world.

(Sutta Nipata, Uragavagga, Mettasutta, chapter 1.8.7-8 verses 148-9)

If you do not attend one another, then who is there to wait upon you?

(Vinaya, Mahavagga chapter 8:26 verse 3)

Those who, seeking their own happiness, punish or kill beings who are also desirous of happiness will not obtain happiness after death.

(The Dhammapada chapter 10 (Punishment) verse 131)

If you want to know what compassion is, look into the eyes of a mother as she cradles her sick and fevered child.

(His Holiness The Dalai Lama)

Whenever you hear that someone else has been successful, rejoice. Always practise your rejoicing for others, whether your friend or your enemy.

(Lama Zopa Rinpoche)

Accustomed long to contemplating love and compassion, I have forgotten all difference between myself and others (non-dualism).

(Milarepa)

Christianity

Love your enemies, do good to those who hate you, bless those who curse you, pray for those who abuse you.

(Luke chapter 6 verses 27-8)

This is my commandment, that you love one another as I have loved you.

(John chapter 15 verse 12)

Rejoice with those who rejoice and weep with those who weep.

(Romans chapter 12 verse 15)

Be you all of one mind, having compassion for one another, love one another, be pitiful, be courteous.

(1 Peter chapter 3 verse 8)

Honour (Care for) your father and mother; which is the first commandment with promise: that it may be well with you and you may live long on the earth.

(Ephesians chapter 6 verses 1-3)

Confucianism

The feeling of distress (at witnessing the suffering of others) is the beginning of humaneness (compassion).

(The Innateness of the Four Great Virtues: Mencius)

Wisdom, humanity (compassion) and courage, these three are the universal virtues.

(The Well-Ordered Society: Doctrine of the Mean)

Hinduism

Be compassionate (*dayadhvam*)...One should practise...compassion.

(The Three Da's: Brhadaranyaka Upanisad)

Compassion towards all living beings.

(Saintly Virtue No. 16 of those endowed with a Divine Nature: Bhagavad-Gita chapter 16 verses 1-3)

Islam

Allah is al-Rahim, the Compassionate, who is gentle and full of compassion.

(The Heights (or The Wall with Elevations) chapter 7 verse 180; Muhammad al-Madani The Ninety-Nine Most Beautiful Names of Allah: No. 30)

The Lord has decreed you should...be kind to your parents... speak unto them words patient and respectful and lower to them the wing of humility out of compassion and say "O Lord, have compassion on them as they raised me up when I was little."

(The Journey by Night chapter 17 verses 23-4)

God has enjoined on humanity to be dutiful and kind to one's parents. Their mothers bear (their children) with hardship. And mothers bring them forth with hardship.

(The Sand Dunes chapter 46 verse 15)

Judaism

Honour your mother and your father.

(The Ten Commandments: Commandment No. 5 Exodus chapter 20 verse 12)

Hearken (Listen) unto your father who begat you and despise not your mother when she is old.

(Proverbs chapter 23 verse 22)

Rejoice not when your enemy falls.

(Proverbs chapter 24 verse 17)

If your enemy is hungry, give them bread to eat; if thirsty, give them water to drink.

(Proverbs chapter 25 verse 21)

Shintoism

Our subjects ever united in loyalty and filial piety have from generation to generation illustrated the beauty of (virtue).

(The Japanese Ethos: Imperial Rescript on Education 30 October 1890 (modernized Shinto))

Taoism

Abandon ostentatious benevolence and conspicuous righteousness, then people will return to the primal virtues of filial piety and parental affection.

(Lao Tzu, Tao Te Ching (Return to Simplicity) chapter 19)

Tao (the Way) has three treasures which one must guard and cherish. The first is called compassion.

(Lao Tzu, Tao Te Ching (Three Treasures) chapter 67)

Compassionate towards yourself, you reconcile all beings in the world.

(Lao Tzu, Tao Te Ching (Three Treasures) chapter 67)

Do not benefit oneself to the harm of others.

(The Chieh Rules)

Those who seek immortality must...rejoice in the fortune of others and pity their suffering.

(The Reward for Deeds: p'ao-p'u Tzu)

Zen Buddhism

Working with deep compassion for all sentient beings...This is what is called Buddha. Do not search beyond it.

(Zen Master Dogen)

Chapter 10

Conscience

Possessing and exercising an inner conscience involves the internal and intuitive recognition of the moral or ethical quality of right and wrong concerning one's actions, omissions and motives. It is paying heed to that quiet but persistent and uncompromising inner voice, the Divine spark within us, when conducting oneself (or contemplating conducting oneself) contrary to the Sacred Scriptures or otherwise behaving inappropriately or unskillfully. We must strive to listen and pay heed to the voice of our soul. Do not suppress these inner whispers by overthinking or over-analyzing the situation or through an exercise in convenient self-justification. The whisperings of the soul want the best for us.

In saintly personalities, exercising the 'overdeveloped' or sensitive conscience is often accompanied by feelings of shame, guilt and remorse. These feelings do serve a purpose in the short term by realigning our souls to the Divine path but must be let go of once they have served such purpose. God is Love, not condemnation; an inner conscience returns us to the Divine path and, once rediscovered, we must forgive ourselves and move forward towards the Light.

Scriptural References

Christianity
I live in all good (clear) conscience before God.
(Acts chapter 23 verse 1)
Have always a conscience void of offence towards God and towards others.
(Acts chapter 24 verse 16)

Confucianism

If you lead the people through virtue and regulate them by the laws of propriety, then they will have a sense of shame (be pricked by their own conscience) and will attain goodness.

(Analects)

The feeling of shame is the beginning of righteousness.

(The Innateness of the Four Great Virtues: Mencius)

Hinduism

Modesty. (*Hrih* means a sense of guilt or shame in performing actions contrary to the injunctions of scriptures and society.)

(Saintly Virtue No. 19 of those endowed with a Divine Nature: Bhagavad-Gita chapter 16 verses 1-3)

Judaism

Wickedness accompanies contempt (shame).

(Proverbs chapter 18 verse 3)

I am ever (on guard) to keep myself free from my sin and guilt.

(Psalms chapter 18 verse 23)

Islam

If you obey and fear God, He will grant you *Furqan* (a conscience or criterion to judge between right and wrong).

(The Spoils chapter 8 verse 29)

The Ten (Native American) Indian Commandments

Do what you know to be right.

(Commandment No. 6)

Zen Buddhism

Do not follow the ideas of others, but learn to listen to the voice within yourself. Your body and mind will become clear and you will realize the unity of all things.

(Dogen)

Chapter 11

Detachment (from the Material World)

"Attachment is the greatest fabricator of illusions; reality can be attained only by someone who is detached" (Simone Weil).

Detachment is the avoidance of attachment to, or separation from, the world and all of its distractions and illusions. It is a letting go. The concept and process of detachment may be variously described. It is an understanding of the relative unimportance and transient nature of personal power, fame, recognition, wealth and luxury and a renunciation of the ways of the world, worldly riches and material objects. It is a letting go of craving, grasping, clinging and distraction (including negative feelings). It is a cessation of desire, obsession and compulsion and a suppression of one's covetousness nature, ego and instinctive sensual appetites. It is a disregard for the ornaments, finery and amusements of the world and abstinence from self-preoccupation, worldly pleasures, prestige and affluence sought by many.

Detachment is the antithesis of a desire to acquire, accumulate and to get one's way all the time. It is a detachment from things which are transitory and impermanent and must be parted with upon death. We enter this world with nothing and depart from it with nothing, apart from those treasures of, and love within, the heart and soul accumulated during one's lifetime. In short, it is living a life of the spirit rather than a worldly or material or sensual one, involving an understanding that worldly opulences are not for personal indulgence but rather to be stewarded in the service of God, humanity and Nature.

Although it is necessary to be in this world, it is not necessary to be of this world. Peace and contentment for the soul come from detachment from the world and its attractions, and through service to others. Although we are neither saints nor saviors and live within a world filled with temptations and distractions, we should try at least to rise above them to the best of our ability and within the bounds of practical constraints. Proceed higher and deeper into the ascending heavens above by releasing whatever attachments you may have to this earthly realm.

Scriptural References

Baha'i

All human beings are earthly; the hearts are connected with this world. Day and night their thoughts and occupations are earthly; all belong to the world. They think about the honors of this world or about the riches and wealth of this world or of name or fame in this world...The Guidance of God makes it evident and plain, when the Way of the Kingdom, the Divine Path, is opened; that this is the road of the Kingdom. It is not sufficient...only to discover the Heavenly Way – you must travel upon it until the end is reached...If you see one whose heart is attached to this world and in whom there is no...detachment or turning to God...then you will know that they are a tree of darkness.

(True Belief: Words of Wisdom from the Supreme Pen of Baha'u'llah)

Buddhism

The cause of suffering is desire (craving).

(The Second Noble Truth)

Verily it is the utter passionless cessation of, the giving up, the forsaking, the release from...craving.

(The First Sermon: Vinaya, Mahavagga)

Do not be devoted to the pleasures of sense which is the way of the world.

(The First Sermon: Vinaya, Mahavagga)

The follower of the law, having forsaken passion and hatred and foolishness, will strive after separation from the world.

(The Dhammapada chapter 1 (The Twin-Verses) verse 20)

Those who have no accumulation (wealth)...whose sphere is emptiness (non-grasping)...their path is difficult to understand (in terms of worldly wisdom), like birds in the sky. Those whose appetites are gone, who are not attached to enjoyment...their path is difficult to understand, like birds in the sky.

(The Dhammapada chapter 7 (The Venerable) verses 92-3)

Come, behold this glittering world, how it resembles an ornamented royal chariot, in which fools flounder, but for the wise there is no attachment to it.

(The Dhammapada chapter 13 (The World) verse 171)

Let us live happily, possessing nothing.

(The Dhammapada chapter 15 (Happiness) verse 200)

Detachment (the extinction of desires and cravings) is the best of states.

(The Dhammapada chapter 19 (The Just) verse 272)

Whosoever in this world is overcome by this fierce thirst (craving for worldly objects), their sorrows grow like the abounding Birana grass.

(The Dhammapada chapter 24 (Thirst) verse 335)

But whosoever overcomes this fierce thirst (craving), sufferings fall away from them like water-drops from a lotus leaf.

(The Dhammapada chapter 24 (Thirst) verse 336)

Led by craving, people run this way and that like an ensnared hare. Therefore let the bhikkhu (Buddhist monk), who wishes for detachment, discard craving.

(The Dhammapada chapter 24 (Thirst) verse 343)

With the relinquishing of all thought and egotism, the enlightened one is liberated through not clinging.

(Majjhima Nikaya chapter 72 verse 15)

Christianity

My (Jesus') kingdom is not of this world.

(John chapter 18 verse 36)

The cares (distractions) of this world and the deceitfulness of riches and the lusts of other things entering in, choke (God's) Word (Law) and it becomes unfruitful.

(Mark chapter 4 verse 19)

Whosoever will come after (follow) me, let them deny themselves (leave self or former worldly ways behind).

(Mark chapter 8 verse 34)

It is easier for a camel to go through the eye of a needle, than for a rich person to enter the Kingdom of God.

(Mark chapter 10 verse 25)

Do not store up for yourselves treasures on earth (material wealth)...but store up for yourselves treasures in heaven (Divine Virtues or spiritual treasures of the heart).

(Matthew chapter 6 verses 19-20)

Keep yourself unspoiled by the world (and its ways).

(James chapter 1 verse 27)

Confucianism

With rough rice to eat and water to drink and one's bent arm to be a pillow, there is still happiness. Riches and reputation if gained dishonorably are just floating clouds.

(Analects)

Hinduism

Renunciation (Detachment).

(Saintly Virtue No. 13 of those endowed with a Divine Nature: Bhagavad-Gita chapter 16 verses 1-3)

Wholly trained in renunciation, released, you will come to God.

(Everything is a Sacrifice to Me: Bhagavad-Gita chapter 9)

Islam

Men are tempted by a life of lusts...of hoarded treasures of gold and silver, of splendid horses, cattle and plantations. These are the enjoyments of this life, but far better is the return to God (entry to Paradise).

(The Family of Imran chapter 3 verse 14)

Every soul must taste death...the life of this world is nothing but the enjoyment of deception (a fleeting vanity or illusory pleasure).

(The Family of Imran chapter 3 verse 185)

The life of this world is nothing but a game and a sport. But far better is the house in the Hereafter (Paradise) for those who are pious.

(The Cattle chapter 6 verse 32)

Avoid those who have taken their faith as a sport and diversion and are deceived by the life of this world.

(The Cattle chapter 6 verse 70)

And truly, you have come to Us (your soul has returned to God) alone (without wealth, companions or anything else) as We created you. You have left behind all that We bestowed on you (during your lifetime).

(The Cattle chapter 6 verse 94)

Know that your...worldly goods are but a temptation and that God's reward is great.

(The Spoils chapter 8 verse 28)

The life of this world as compared with the Hereafter is but a brief passing enjoyment.

(The Thunder chapter 13 verse 26)

Those who prefer the life of this world to the Hereafter...are far astray from God.

((Prophet) Abraham chapter 14 verse 3)

Your worldly goods are transitory, but what God has endures.

(The Bees chapter 16 verse 96)

Do not desire the adornment of the life of this world.

(The Cave chapter 18 verse 28)

Wealth and children are an adornment of the life of this world. But enduring righteous deeds are better rewarded by God and hold for you a greater hope of salvation.

(The Cave chapter 18 verse 46)

The life of this world is but a sport and a play. It is the life to come (the Hereafter) that is the true life: if they but knew it.

(The Spider chapter 29 verse 64)

Whatever you have been given is but a fleeting enjoyment for this worldly life, but that which is with God (Paradise) is better and more lasting for those who believe.

(The Counsel chapter 42 verse 36)

Know that the life of this world is but...a play and an empty boast among you, a rivalry for greater riches...The life of this world is only an illusory pleasure.

(Iron chapter 57 verse 20)

God is better than diversion (amusement) and merchandise (material possessions).

(The Congregation chapter 62 verse 11)

Humanity is truly excessive in the love of (worldly) wealth.

(The Charging Steeds chapter 100 verse 8)

The mutual rivalry for piling up of worldly things deludes you until you die...If you knew with a sure knowledge the end result of piling up or accumulating, you would not have occupied yourselves in worldly things.

(Contention About Numbers chapter 102 verses 1-5)

Jainism

I renounce all attachments, whether...small or great.

(Fifth Great Vow: Acaranga Sutra)

Those who indulge in worldly pleasures are born again and again.

(Acaranga Sutra: Fourth Lecture First Lesson: Righteousness)

Conquer the passions which defile the soul: wrath, pride,

deceit and greed.

(Sutrakrtanga: Book 1 Sixth Lecture: Praise of Mahavira)

Fame, glory and renown; honours and respectful treatment; all pleasures in the whole world: from all this a wise person should abstain.

(Sutrakrtanga: Book 1 Ninth Lecture: The Law)

A sage should wander about free from all worldly ties.

(Sutrakrtanga: Book 1 Tenth Lecture: Carefulness)

After a virtuous beginning, some become miserable and lose heart, desiring honour and fame.

(Sutrakrtanga: Book 1 Tenth Lecture: Carefulness)

A pious monk, free from bonds (attachments), should wander about desiring neither honour nor fame.

(Sutrakrtanga: Book 1 Tenth Lecture: Carefulness)

If a monk is attached to vanities and desires fame, they will suffer again and again in the Circle of Births.

(Sutrakrtanga: Book 1 Thirteenth Lecture: The Real Truth)

Cast aside from you all attachments, as the lotus lets drop the pure monsoon water.

(The Simile of the Leaf: Uttaradhyayana)

I renounce...all passions, attachment, aversion, fear, sorrow, joy, anxiety, self-pity...all these I abandon with body, mind and speech.

(The Lay Person's Inner Voyage: Nityanaimittika-pathavali)

Though one believes in the Law, it will rarely be practised; for people are engrossed by worldly pleasures.

(The Simile of the Leaf: Uttaradhyayana)

Give up...the large fortune you have amassed; do not desire it a second time.

(The Simile of the Leaf: Uttaradhyayana)

Wealth will not protect a careless person in this world and the next.

(Impurity: Uttaradhyayana)

Judaism

There are those who make themselves (materially) rich, yet have nothing (spiritually): there are those who make themselves poor (through giving), yet have great riches (of the heart).

(Proverbs chapter 13 verse 7)

Those who love (worldly) pleasure shall be poor (lacking in spiritual awareness and treasures).

(Proverbs chapter 21 verse 17)

Sikhism

O God, save us from the sin of attachment.

(The Community and its Past Saints: A Congregational Prayer)

Worldly love.

(One of five Sikh deadly sins)

Taoism

Do not get involved in things (distractions) and lose sight of the Tao (the Way, the Truth or Universal Energy, Laws or Principles).

(The Chieh Rules)

They who are eternally without worldly desire perceive the spiritual side.

(Lao Tzu, Tao Te Ching (What is the Tao) chapter 1)

Ignoring the things which awaken desire keeps the heart undisturbed.

(Lao Tzu, Tao Te Ching (Quieting People) chapter 3)

Diminish desire.

(Lao Tzu, Tao Te Ching (Return to Simplicity) chapter 19)

Let all...hold to that which is reliable, namely...reduce one's possessions.

(Lao Tzu, Tao Te Ching (Return to Simplicity) chapter 19)

There is no calamity greater than acquisitiveness (fondness for acquiring possessions).

(Lao Tzu, Tao Te Ching (Limitation of Desire) chapter 46)
To have wealth and treasure in abundance is to know the pride of robbers.

(Lao Tzu, Tao Te Ching (Gain by Insight) chapter 53)
Not grasping after things (the wise person) does not lose them.

(Lao Tzu, Tao Te Ching (Consider the Insignificant) chapter 64)
By letting it go it gets all done. The world is won by those who let it go.

(Lao Tzu)

Zen Buddhism

We accept the graceful falling of mountain cherry blossoms. But it is much harder for us to fall away from our attachment to the world.

(Zen Wisdom)

Zoroastrianism

You should not become presumptuous through much treasure and wealth; for in the end it is necessary for you to leave all.

(Commandments for the Body and the Soul)

Let the world...be taught not to set their hearts on the pleasures and vanities of life, as nothing can be carried away with them (into the Hereafter)...In (the prime of) youth, when blessed with health and vigour, you suppose that your strength will never fail; that your riches, your lands, your houses and your honours will remain for ever...But, O Arda-Viraf! Teach them not to think so: teach them the danger of such a way of thinking: all, all will pass away as a dream! The flowers fade and give lessons unto (humanity) that they are unwilling to profit by. Yea, the world itself will pass away and nothing will remain but God!

(The Vision of Arda-Viraf)

(The Prophet) Zarathustra (Zoroaster) asked Ahura-Mazda (God): "O thou all-knowing Ahura-Mazda, should I urge upon the godly (remind the righteous)...that they have once to leave behind them the earth made by Ahura, that they have to leave... their wealth?" Ahura-Mazda answered: "Thou should, O holy Zarathustra."

(Reward for the Pious)

Chapter 12

Devotional Prayer (Worship) and Piety

Prayer transcends religion. Prayer is the worship of, and the cultivation of a devout spiritual communion with, God. It often includes a petition, invocation or supplication to God. To pray is to surrender or submit oneself and one's anxieties and concerns humbly, obediently and completely to God's will and to totally depend on His providential care. "Prayer is putting oneself in the hands of God, at His disposition and listening to His voice in the depth of our hearts" (Mother Teresa). When we submit to God, our hearts are opened to Divine love, casting out our fear of the unknown. When we surrender to Heaven, we trust that all of our needs, material and spiritual, will be provided for by a benevolent and loving God.

Prayer also enhances one's reverence of, and hunger and thirst for, God, nourishing the soul by creating a sacred bond between God and the soul for imparting Divine knowledge. Devotional and meditative prayer reveals the presence of God within and through all things (immanence and omnipresence) and offers up the opportunity to develop a loving and intimate relationship with the Divine, indeed to become one with, and absorbed into, God (the subsuming of individual consciousness into the All-consciousness of God).

Attitude to prayer may be differentiated from the means or method of prayer. Right attitude includes one of loving devotion and reverence/piety towards God. It also involves a sense of remembrance, gratitude, rejoicing and thankfulness for His bountiful and countless gifts and blessings in our lives (life, family, education, skills, talents, health, opportunities, enough food to eat, a roof over our head and so forth), as well as an expression of awe at the deep, ineffable and ungraspable nature or essence of the Divine. Such gratitude deepens our prayers and opens our 'spiritual' heart to receive the Divine Virtues. "Gratitude bestows reverence, allowing us to encounter everyday epiphanies, those transcendent moments of awe that change forever how we experience life and the world" (John Milton). As to means, prayer may be undertaken as part of a community-based congregation of worshippers in which praise and glory are offered up, or alone in a private or secluded place or sanctuary. In the latter context, individual daily offerings may be performed or contemplative/meditative prayer undertaken to still the soul and meditate lovingly on the Divine, focussing, for example, on the qualities and attributes of God and His infinite nature or expressing gratitude for His abundant gifts and blessings in our life.

Prayer must have a disciplined focus on God and emanate from a pure, sincere and undivided, rather than hypocritical, heart. Without sincerity, religious rituals and rites are largely meaningless. God does not require sophisticated, beautifully-crafted and elegant words and phrases from the mind, but simple, trusting and childlike prayers from the heart. Silence your inner self so that you may hear God more clearly. Prayer must also be undertaken with full confidence and faith that God hears our prayers and will grant our petitions in the fullness of His (not our) time. All things will come at their appointed time (I Ching). God is always on time; it is we who lack patience and perseverance. Our prayers should therefore be of an affirmative and faithful nature, thanking God as if our prayers have already been answered.

Scriptural References

Baha'i
Be reverent towards God.
(The Commands of the Blessed Master Abdul-Baha)
Remember Me (God) in My earth, that I may remember you

in My Heaven.

(Of Divine Humanity: Words of Wisdom from the Supreme Pen of Baha'u'llah)

Be content in Me and thankful to Me.

(Of Divine Humanity: Words of Wisdom from the Supreme Pen of Baha'u'llah)

If you love Me, turn away from yourself; if My Will you seek, regard not your own; that you may die in Me and I live in you.

(Of Divine Humanity: Words of Wisdom from the Supreme Pen of Baha'u'llah)

Every day in the morning when arising...If you see your belief (faith) is stronger and your heart more occupied with God and your love increased and your freedom from the world greater; then thank God and ask for the increase of these qualities.

(True Belief: Words of Wisdom from the Supreme Pen of Baha'u'llah)

The healer of all your troubles is remembrance of God; forget it not.

(Of the Light: Words of Wisdom from the Supreme Pen of Baha'u'llah)

To the state of holiness I call you; abide in it, that you may be in peace for ever.

(Of the Light: Words of Wisdom from the Supreme Pen of Baha'u'llah)

Buddhism

Like a beautiful flower that is full of color but without scent, even so are the fine but fruitless words of one who does not practise them.

(The Dhammapada chapter 4 (Flowers) verse 51)

To dwell on the highest thoughts (consciousness-raising), this is the teaching of the Awakened.

(The Dhammapada chapter 14 (The Buddha/The Awakened) verse 185)

Christianity

Whatsoever (the scribes and the Pharisees) bid you observe, that observe and do, but do not follow after their works: for they say and do not.

(Matthew chapter 23 verse 3)

Ask and it shall be given you; seek and you shall find; knock and it shall be opened unto you. For every one who asks receives and every one who seeks finds and to every one who knocks it shall be opened. If a child shall ask bread of any of you who is a parent, will the parent give a stone?...If you then, being evil, know how to give good gifts unto your children: how much more shall your heavenly Father give the Holy Spirit to those who ask Him?

(Luke chapter 11 verses 9-13)

Do not lay up earthly treasure for yourself, but be rich in prayer and love towards God.

(Luke chapter 12 verse 21)

God is a spirit: and they who worship Him must worship Him in spirit and in truth.

(John chapter 4 verse 24)

Ask and you shall receive, that your joy may be full.

(John chapter 16 verse 24)

I make a decisive dedication of my body as a living sacrifice, holy and well pleasing to God.

(Romans chapter 12 verse 1)

I...offer to God pleasing service and...worship, with modesty and pious care and godly fear and awe.

(Hebrews chapter 12 verse 28)

Submit yourselves...to God.

(James chapter 4 verse 7)

Rejoice in the Lord always.

(Philippians chapter 4 verse 4)

In everything by prayer and supplication with thanksgiving let your requests be made known unto God.

(Philippians chapter 4 verse 6)

Cicero

Gratitude is not only the greatest of virtues, but the parent of all others.

(Cicero)

Desiderata

Be at peace with God, whatever you conceive Him to be...and keep peace with your soul.

(Verse 17)

Hinduism

By meditating upon God, desire is satisfied.

(Svetasvatara Upanisad)

Whoso loves and worships God, to God will that person come indeed.

(Bhakti and the Availability of God: Bhagavad-Gita chapter 7)

Great souls resort to God, to Divine nature, thinking of no one else, they worship Me...revering Me in their devotion, constant in discipline, in reverence they know Me.

(Everything is a Sacrifice to Me: Bhagavad-Gita chapter 9)

When you offer with love a leaf, a flower or water to Me, I accept that offer of love from the giver who gives of oneself.

(Everything is a Sacrifice to Me: Bhagavad-Gita chapter 9)

If they (those who make offerings) worship me lovingly, they are in me and I in them.

(Everything is a Sacrifice to Me: Bhagavad-Gita chapter 9)

Worship and love Me! Think of Me. Be devoted to Me. Revere Me while making an offering to Me. Thus disciplining yourself, wholly intent on Me, you will come to Me.

(Everything is a Sacrifice to Me: Bhagavad-Gita chapter 9)

Who loves Me without other desires and has no ill will towards any creatures at all, they come to Me.

(Bhagavad-Gita)

Islam

Praise belongs to God, the Lord of the worlds, the Merciful, the Compassionate.

(The Opening chapter 1 verse 2)

Devote (resign or surrender) yourself to the Lord of all worlds.

(The Cow chapter 2 verse 131)

Remember God and God will remember you and be grateful to God.

(The Cow chapter 2 verse 152)

God responds to the prayerful petitions of the believers when they call on Him.

(The Cow chapter 2 verse 186)

God is my Lord and your Lord, so worship Him. This is the right path.

(The Family of Imran chapter 3 verse 51)

God will reward the grateful.

(The Family of Imran chapter 3 verse 144)

Remember God...and reflect on the creation of the heavens and the earth.

(The Family of Imran chapter 3 verse 191)

Serve God and join none with Him (in worship).

(The Women chapter 4 verse 36)

The hypocrites...pray for the sake of ostentation and remember God but little.

(The Women chapter 4 verse 142)

Pray to your Lord humbly and secretly.

(The Heights (or the Wall with Elevations) chapter 7 verse 55)

Remember your Lord deep in your soul humbly and with reverential awe and without ostentation: in the morning and in the evening and do not be neglectful.

(The Heights (or the Wall with Elevations) chapter 7 verse 205)

God loves the pious.

(The Repentance chapter 9 verse 4)

In the remembrance of God shall the hearts of believers find peace and be comforted.

(The Thunder chapter 13 verse 28)

Verily, God surely hears all prayers.

((Prophet) Abraham chapter 14 verse 39)

There is none in the heavens or on earth but shall return to the Merciful God in submission.

(Mary chapter 19 verse 93)

Those who are with God are never too proud to worship Him, nor are they ever wearied. They praise Him night and day tirelessly.

(The Prophets chapter 21 verses 19-20)

Come before God with a heart devoted to Him.

(The Poets chapter 26 verse 89)

God is full of grace for humanity, but most...do not give thanks.

(The Ants chapter 27 verse 73)

Be steadfast in prayer. Prayer fends off sin and wrong.

(The Spider chapter 29 verse 45)

God answer the prayers of those who believe and do righteous deeds and gives them increase of His grace.

(The Counsel chapter 42 verse 26)

Do not say with your tongue what is not in your heart.

(The Victory chapter 48 verse 11)

O you who believe! Let not your wealth or your children divert you from the remembrance of God.

(The Hypocrites chapter 63 verse 9)

Whatsoever is in the heavens and whatsoever is on the earth glorifies God. His is the kingdom and to Him belong all the praises...He it is Who created you...He created the heavens and the earth in truth.

(Cheating chapter 64 verses 1-3)

Surely humanity was created fretful (anxiety-ridden), when evil exists, very impatient, when good visits, niggardly, save those who...continue at their prayers, those in whose wealth is a right known for the beggar and the outcast (those who joyfully make a loan to Allah by giving charity to His poor)...Those who observe their prayers shall be in Gardens [of Paradise], high-honoured.

(The Ways of Ascent chapter 70 verses 19-35)

Woe to those who pray and...make display and refuse charity.

(The Small Kindnesses chapter 107 verses 4-7)

Judaism

Love the Lord your God with all your heart and with all your soul and with all your strength.

(Deuteronomy chapter 6 verses 4-7)

Give unto the Lord the glory due to His name; worship the Lord in the beauty of holiness.

(Psalms chapter 29 verse 2)

It is a good thing to give thanks unto the Lord and to sing praises unto Your name, O most High. To show forth Your loving-kindness in the morning and Your faithfulness every night.

(Psalms chapter 92 verses 1-2)

Bless the Lord, O my soul; and all that is within me, bless His holy name...Forget not all His benefits. Who forgives all your iniquities; Who heals all your diseases. Who redeems your life from destruction; Who crowns you with lovingkindness and tender mercies.

(Psalms chapter 103 verses 1-4)

Bless the Lord, O my soul! O Lord my God, You are very great!...Bless the Lord, O my soul! Praise the Lord.

(Psalms chapter 104 verses 1 and 35)

Praise the Lord! For the Lord is good; sing praises to His name, for He is gracious.

(Psalms chapter 135 verse 3)

The Lord is near unto all those who call upon Him, to all who call upon Him sincerely and in truth.

(Psalms chapter 145 verse 18)

You shall pray unto God and He shall hear you.

(Job chapter 22 verse 27)

Perfect Liberty Kyodan (Modernized Shinto)

Depend on God at all times.

(Twenty-One Precepts: No. 11)

Shintoism

At festivals we serve the deities by purifying ourselves, with sincerity revere the dignity of the deities, return thanks for their benefits and offer earnest prayers.

(Purity and Awe: Kokutai no Hongi)

Sikhism

Piety.

(One of five Sikh Virtues)

I take the formless God into my heart and there make obeisance unto Him.

(From the Akal Ustat: Praise of the Immortal)

What pleases God is real (authentic/sincere) worship.

(From the Sohila: Guru Nanak)

The hunger of the hungry for God does not subside.

(God as Truth: Guru Nanak's Japji)

At the ambrosial hour of morning meditate on the true Name and God's greatness.

(God as Truth: Guru Nanak's Japji)

Put God's love into your hearts...and you shall be absorbed in Him who is the abode of happiness.

(God as Truth: Guru Nanak's Japji)

Let me lose myself in (become one with) God.

(Spiritual Marriage: The Bara Mah)

Only those who love God conquer love of self.

(Spiritual Marriage: The Bara Mah)

Numberless Thy silent worshippers who lovingly fix their thoughts upon Thee.

(The Repetition of the Divine Name: The Japji)

Taoism

Take time to...worship the unnameable and to embrace the unformed (the Tao).

(Lao Tzu and the Hua Hu Ching)

The Ten (Native American) Indian Commandments

Remain close to the Great Spirit (God).

(Commandment No. 2)

When you arise in the morning, give thanks for the morning light. Give thanks for life and strength. Give thanks for your food. And give thanks for the joy of living. And if perchance you see no reason to give thanks, rest assured the fault is yours.

(Native American Indian proverb attributed to Tecumseh)

Zoroastrianism

God...requires only two things of humanity: the first, that they should not sin; the next, that they shall be grateful of the many blessings He is continually bestowing upon them.

(The Vision of Arda-Viraf)

Abide by the Laws (Commandments of God) and walk in the way of Truth and holiness and continue in the worship of the true God.

(The Vision of Arda-Viraf)

The life of a man is of short duration and many troubles and anxieties fall to his lot; and a man, after fifty years of prosperity and happiness, may be, by some unforeseen event, reduced to sickness and poverty. Many are tried by this criterion and but few are found worthy. To suffer a day of pain, after fifty years of pleasure, is too much for them and they complain in bitterness of spirit to the Creator of all good of His injustice and cruelty, without remembering the good they have so long enjoyed.

(The Vision of Arda-Viraf)

Praises and songs and adorations do we offer to Ahura-Mazda (God)...And to Thy good kingdom, O Ahura-Mazda! may we attain for ever and a good King be Thou over us.

(God as the King, the Life, The Rewarder)

Chapter 13

Faith

"Faith is the substance of things hoped for; the evidence of things not seen" (New Testament: Hebrews chapter 11 verses 1 and 3). Faith is belief in something which is not based on proof or which cannot be seen or perceived by the ordinary senses (sense-perception). It is a profoundly intuitive certainty of knowledge of the existence of something which cannot be proven objectively, scientifically or empirically.

In the religious and spiritual contexts, pure faith presupposes an absolute, constant, unqualified and unconditional genuine belief in the existence of, and trust in, God, which admits of no doubt, questioning, wavering or exceptions, as God's Will and ways cannot be questioned. Such a faith is based on a deeply personal and intimate relationship with the Divine in which one loses oneself to faith for salvation. Faith resides in the heart and is strengthened by good deeds and righteous works. In complete confidence, reliance and conviction, when we humbly petition God, we know our prayers have already been answered, perhaps not immediately or when we desire, but in God's time and in His manner (or, to put it otherwise, when our personal circumstances are ripe for receipt of the blessing). Although the petitioner or supplicant proposes, it is God Who disposes. Therefore, lean not unto your own understanding (Proverbs chapter 3 verse 5) but commit your burdens to God. Rest assured that you are deeply loved, known and cherished by the Creator.

Faith is particularly important for us when difficult events or circumstances arise in our lives, including those caused by others and we earnestly search without success for an explanation or reason, but intuitively knowing deep down that nothing in the

Universe is accidental, that everything which happens is for a reason and for our spiritual growth and that all will ultimately be revealed, not in our time but in God's time, and that God is always with us. Such faith will restore our faith in humanity.

Scriptural References

Baha'i

Empty yourselves of doubts...that you may be prepared for Eternal Life and ready to meet God. Herein there is no death, no trouble or burden.

(Of the Light: Words of Wisdom from the Supreme Pen of Baha'u'llah)

Humanity is ever degraded by ignorance, lack of faith, untruth and selfishness.

(Of Knowledge: Words of Wisdom from the Supreme Pen of Baha'u'llah)

True Belief is not only to acknowledge the Oneness of God. By belief we mean that the reality of a person will be characterized by Divine characteristics. If their reality is dark, they will become enlightened. If they are heedless they will become conscious; if they are sleeping, they will be awakened; if they are earthly, they will become heavenly...This is the meaning of true belief.

(True Belief: Words of Wisdom from the Supreme Pen of Baha'u'llah)

Buddhism

The wise do not befriend the faithless.

(Udanavarga Chapter 25 Verse 1)

Christianity

If you have faith the size of a mustard seed...nothing will be impossible for you.

(Matthew chapter 17 verse 20)

Have faith in God...Whatever things you desire, when you pray, believe that you will receive them and you shall have them.

(Mark chapter 11 verses 22-4)

Consider the lilies how they grow: they toil not, they spin not; and yet I say unto you, that Solomon in all his glory was not arrayed as one of these. If then God so clothe the grass, which is today in the field and tomorrow is cast into the fire; how much more will He clothe you, O you of little faith? And seek not what you shall eat, or what you shall drink, neither be of doubtful mind. For all these things do the nations of the world seek after: and your Father knows that you have need of these things. But rather seek the kingdom of God; and all these things shall be added unto you.

(Luke chapter 12 verses 27-31)

The things which are impossible (for humanity) are possible with God.

(Luke chapter 18 verse 27)

Blessed are they who have not seen and yet have believed.

(John chapter 20 verse 29)

Your faith should not be based on the wisdom of (human philosophy), but in the power of God.

(1 Corinthians chapter 2 verse 5)

I live by faith, not by sight (sense-perception).

(2 Corinthians chapter 5 verse 7)

Faith, if it does not have works (supporting charitable and righteous deeds), is dead.

(James chapter 2 verse 17)

Faith is the substance of things hoped for, the evidence of things not seen...Through faith we understand that the worlds were framed by the Word of God, so that things which are seen were not made of things which do appear (the material realm was created by the unseen or incorporeal God).

(Hebrews chapter 11 verses 1 and 3)

Without faith it is impossible to please God and those who come to Him must believe that He exists and that He is a rewarder of those who diligently seek Him.

(Hebrews chapter 11 verse 6)

Hinduism

Those of wisdom put their trust in God alone and resign (submit or surrender) themselves to God.

(Bhakti and the Availability of God: Bhagavad-Gita Chapter 7)

Islam

Those who exchange faith for disbelief have strayed far from the right path.

(The Cow chapter 2 verse 108)

Put your trust in God. God loves those who put their trust in Him.

(The Family of Imran chapter 3 verse 159)

Those who believe in God and hold fast to Him, He will admit them to His Mercy and Grace and guide them to Himself on a straight path.

(The Women chapter 4 verse 175)

Do not say that you believe with your mouth when your heart does not believe.

(The Table chapter 5 verse 41)

Avoid those who take their religion for a play and a sport and whom the life of this world has deceived.

(The Cattle chapter 6 verse 70)

God is our Lord and upon God believers put all their trust.

(The Repentance chapter 9 verse 51)

There is no god but God; upon Him do I rely and unto Him is my repentance.

(The Thunder chapter 13 verse 30)

Some profess to serve God and yet waiver in their faith. When blessed with good fortune they are content, but when a trial befalls them they turn upon their heels (their faith dissipates), losing this life and the next.

(The Pilgrimage chapter 22 verse 11)

God is the Protector of those who believe.

(The Fighting chapter 47 verse 11)

God has endeared the Faith to you and has beautified it in your hearts and has made disbelief, wickedness and disobedience (to God's Commandments) hateful to you. Such are they who are rightly guided.

(The Inner Chambers chapter 49 verse 7)

God has written Faith in the hearts of the believers.

(The Wrangler chapter 58 verse 22)

Whosoever believes in God and performs righteous good deeds, He will expiate from them their sins and will admit them to (Paradise), to dwell therein forever.

(Cheating chapter 64 verse 9)

Whosoever believes in God, He guides their heart, for God knows all things.

(Cheating chapter 64 verse 11)

Verily, those who have reverential awe towards God in private, for them is forgiveness and a great reward (Paradise).

(The Kingdom chapter 67 verse 12)

The faith that has most virtue is that you shall recognize that God is with you wherever you may be.

(Hadith from Muhammad Haqqi al-Nazili's Khazinat al-Asrar)

Judaism

The righteous shall live by their faith.

(Habakkuk chapter 2 verse 4)

Trust in the Lord with all your heart and lean not unto your own understanding.

(Proverbs chapter 3 verse 5)

The heart devises one's way: but the Lord directs the steps of the believer (Humanity proposes but God disposes).

(Proverbs chapter 16 verse 9)

Whoso trusts in the Lord shall be safe.

(Proverbs chapter 29 verse 25)

The Lord...knows those who take refuge and trust in Him.

(Nahum chapter 1 verse 7)

I trust in, rely on and am confident in You, O Lord; You are my God. My times are in Your hands.

(Psalms chapter 31 verses 14-15)

I trust in God at all times. I pour out my heart before Him; God is a refuge for me.

(Psalms chapter 62 verse 8)

Sikhism

Meditate on the true Name and God's greatness...by His favour we shall reach the gate of salvation...we shall thus know that God is altogether true.

(God as Truth: Guru Nanak's Japji)

Exceedingly fortunate are those of God who have faith in Him and thirst for Him.

(From the Rahiras: Guru Ram Das)

Preserve the faith and remove doubt from our hearts; save us, O Formless One!

(Prayer by Guru Arjan)

Grant to Thy Sikhs...the gift of faith.

(Sri Wahguru Ji Ki Fatah!)

Without good works no one can be saved (No amount of meditation or worship can atone for faith without righteous deeds).

(Guru Nanak)

Taoism

If one's faith fails, no reward of faith will be received.

(Lao Tzu, Tao Te Ching (Emptiness and Not-Doing (*Wu Wei*)) chapter 23)

When rulers lack faith, you may seek in vain for it among their subjects.

(Lao Tzu, Tao Te Ching (Simplicity of Habit) chapter 17)

Zoroastrianism

To attain God's friendship you must walk in His ways and place in Him the firmest reliance. The provisions (requisite for the journey to eternal life) must be faith and hope and the remembrance of your good works.

(The Vision of Arda-Viraf)

Chapter 14

Fearlessness (Courage)

Fear is a distressed feeling of impending threat or difficulty or anxiety. While fear, anxiety and worry are a natural and understandable part of the human condition, they remain irrational, futile and negative emotions and, as such, diminish within each of our souls the unconditional and original love we entered this world with. Fear often arises over undue attachment to those things we cherish most and the fear of being separated from them. Fear is also begotten through ignorance and separation and uncertainty as to what the future holds for us. Fear and anxiety impede progress along our spiritual path and hold us back from becoming what God wants for our soul – our development into the best version of ourselves. Although we may feel separated and distant from God, God is never separated and distant from us.

Fearlessness and courage are Divine Virtues esteemed particularly by the Abrahamic religions (Judaism, Christianity and Islam). They are the antitheses of fear and aversion and are associated or correlated with love of, and faith in, God and trust in His providential care and that He is always with us. Fearlessness is release from anxiety or concern over current problems or perceived future difficulties; courage is the quality of mind that enables one to face difficulties without fear. The Holy Scriptures enjoin believers not to worry as there is really nothing to fear. Detachment from the illusions of the world and trust and faith in, and love of, and surrender to, God drive fear from the heart. Therefore, dispel fear and doubt therefrom by restraining the whisperings and promptings of your inner ego. "Perfect love casts out fear" (New Testament: 1 John chapter 4 verse 18). As the sage proverb says, it is best to live one day at a time and to cherish each day to the fullest. We truly have nothing to fear as God knows what we need and bestows upon us accordingly.

Scriptural References

Buddhism
May fear and dread not conquer me.
(Majjhima Nikaya chapter 6 verse 8)
I rejoice free from fear.
(Majjhima Nikaya chapter 92 verses 17 and 19)

Christianity
Which of you by taking thought (worry or anxiety) can add one cubit unto one's stature?
(Matthew chapter 6 verse 27)
Take no thought about what we shall eat or what we shall drink or what clothes we shall wear...But seek first the kingdom of God and His righteousness; and all these things shall be added unto you. Take therefore no thought for tomorrow, for tomorrow shall have worries of its own. Sufficient for each day is its own trouble.
(Matthew chapter 6 verses 31, 33-34)
Why are you so fearful? How is it that you have no faith?
(Mark chapter 4 verse 40)
Let not your heart be troubled, neither let it be afraid.
(John chapter 14 verse 27)
Cast all your cares (anxieties, worries and concerns) on (God); for He cares for you.
(1 Peter chapter 5 verse 7)
I will not fear what people shall do to me.
(Hebrews chapter 13 verse 6)
There is no fear in love; but perfect love casts out fear...One who fears is not made perfect in love.
(1 John chapter 4 verse 18)

God has not given me a spirit of fear and timidity, but of power, love and self-discipline.

(2 Timothy chapter 1 verse 7)

Confucianism

Wisdom, humanity (compassion) and courage, these three are the universal virtues.

(The Well-Ordered Society: Doctrine of the Mean)

Desiderata

Do not distress yourself with imaginings. Many fears are born of fatigue and loneliness.

(Verses 13-14)

Hinduism

Fearlessness.

(Saintly Virtue No. 1 of those endowed with a Divine Nature: Bhagavad-Gita chapter 16 verses 1-3)

Islam

Nothing shall befall us but what God has prescribed for us; He is our Lord; in God let the believers put all their trust.

(The Repentance chapter 9 verse 51)

So many a creature carries not its own sustenance! God provides for it and for you.

(The Spider chapter 29 verse 60)

Judaism

I fear not and am not in terror, for it is the Lord my God who goes with me.

(Deuteronomy chapter 31 verse 6)

I am not afraid, neither am I dismayed, for the Lord my God is with me wherever I go.

(Joshua chapter 1 verse 9)

I am strong and courageous. I am not afraid or discouraged, because the Lord my God is with me.

(2 Chronicles chapter 32 verses 7-8)

I fear not, for God is with me. I do not look around in terror and be dismayed, for He is my God. He will strengthen...me.

(Isaiah chapter 41 verse 10)

Yes, though I walk through the valley of the shadow of death, I will fear no evil, for You are with me; Your rod and Your staff, they comfort me.

(Psalms chapter 23 verse 4)

The Lord is my Light and my Salvation – whom shall I fear or dread? The Lord is the refuge and stronghold of my life – of whom shall I be afraid?

(Psalms chapter 27 verse 1)

When I am afraid, I will trust in You. In God, whose word I praise, in God I trust; I will not be afraid. What can others do to me?

(Psalms chapter 56 verses 3-4)

Sikhism

All fear has departed from those who meditate on the fearless God.

(From the Rahiras: Guru Ram Das)

God provides everyone with their daily food; why...are you afraid? The kulang flies away hundreds of miles, leaving her young behind her. Who feeds them? Who gives them morsels to peck at? Have you not considered this?

(From the Rahiras: Guru Arjan)

Taoism

Courage restrained by caution leads to life.

(Lao Tzu, Tao Te Ching (Action is Dangerous) chapter 73)

Chapter 15

Fear of God (Reverential Awe/Wonder)

An apparent limited exception to the Virtue of Fearlessness, namely Fear or Reverential Awe of God, in itself a Divine Virtue, may be found in the Holy Scriptures of some faiths including the Abrahamic religions, particularly Judaism and Islam. While the notion of fearing what has been described in an earlier chapter as the God of unconditional Love and Compassion and Forgiveness may sound paradoxical and counterintuitive, in this context, fear does not mean dread or recoiling terror but rather a reverential and loving awe and wonder and mindfulness towards God.

While love of God and respect for Divine proscriptions constitute more positive reasons for obedience to His will, the 'Abrahamic' fear of God and the negative consequences for the soul of violating those proscriptions have much the same aim and effect; that is, to prevent sin and wrongdoing by obeying God's Commandments and to encourage the believer to reflect on any transgressions committed. There is an obvious connection here with the Divine Virtue of Conscience discussed previously. In Judaism (Proverbs/Psalms), fear of the Lord is considered the beginning of Divine knowledge, wisdom and understanding (Divine Virtues in themselves which will be analyzed later).

Scriptural References

Baha'i
The fear of God is the real guardian and the ideal protector.
(Tablet of the Word: Baha'u'llah)

Christianity
Fear God.

(1 Peter chapter 2 verse 17)

I...offer to God pleasing service and...worship, with...Godly fear and awe.

(Hebrews chapter 12 verse 28)

Let us cleanse ourselves from all filthiness of the flesh and spirit, perfecting holiness in the fear of God.

(2 Corinthians chapter 7 verse 1)

Islam

For those who believe and fear God, there is a great reward.

(The Family of Imran chapter 3 verse 179)

God shall provide mercy for those who are God-fearing.

(The Heights (or The Wall with Elevations) chapter 7 verse 156)

Believers, fear God and stand with those who uphold the cause of Truth.

(The Repentance chapter 9 verse 119)

God is with those who fear Him.

(The Bees chapter 16 verse 128)

Those who walk in the fear of the Lord...who give alms with hearts filled with awe...shall be first to attain salvation.

(The Believers chapter 23 verse 60)

Judaism

Fear the Lord your God...keep all His statutes and His commandments.

(Deuteronomy chapter 6 verse 2)

You...shall fear your God: I am the Lord.

(Leviticus chapter 19 verse 14)

Fear of the Lord is the beginning of (Divine) knowledge.

(Proverbs chapter 1 verse 7)

Be not wise in your own eyes: but reverently fear the Lord and depart from evil.

(Proverbs chapter 3 verse 7)

Fear of the Lord is the beginning of wisdom.

(Proverbs chapter 9: verse 10)

The fear of the Lord is a fountain of life, to depart from the snares of death (evil/sin).

(Proverbs chapter 14 verse 27)

Better is little with the fear of the Lord than great treasure and trouble therewith.

(Proverbs chapter 15 verse 16)

By the fear of the Lord one departs from evil.

(Proverbs chapter 16 verse 6)

By humility and the fear of the Lord are riches (treasures of the heart) and honour and life.

(Proverbs chapter 22 verse 4)

I will worship...at the Lord's holy temple in reverent fear and awe of Him.

(Psalms chapter 5 verse 7)

The fear of the Lord is the beginning of wisdom: a good understanding have all they who obey God's Commandments.

(Psalms chapter 111 verse 10)

The Lord will fulfil the desires of those who fear Him: He also will hear their cry and will save them.

(Psalms chapter 145 verse 19)

Chapter 16

Forgiveness (Mercy) and Reconciliation

As the oft-cited proverb says, to err is human; to forgive is Divine. Forgiveness is the magnanimous granting of a free and unqualified pardon for an offence or transgression committed against us. It is not the condoning of the transgression itself. It is the capacity and willingness to overlook the wrongdoing committed by others without holding a grudge or feeling resentment or the need to retaliate or take revenge. It is the sending of love and compassion to the transgressor and praying for their soul. Indeed, it has been said that it is a soul's glory to pass over a transgression (Proverbs chapter 19 verse 11). Forgiveness facilitates reconciliation (a poignant and moving example of which is the parable of the Lost or Prodigal Son in the New Testament: Luke chapter 15).

By expressing forgiveness, our emotional wounds caused by the wrongdoing begin to heal. We begin to cease living in the past and move towards living life more fully in the preciousness of the present moment. When you forgive, you heal; when you let go, you grow (Zen proverb). Though forgiveness may be very difficult, indeed virtually impossible, in certain circumstances, it is something the Holy Scriptures (particularly of the Abrahamic religions and especially in Christianity in the context of the Lord's Prayer) call upon believers to do, if they desire for God in turn to forgive them for their wrongdoing. In short, mercy is at the heart of the Divine Law.

And do not forget to be forgiving of yourself. Many of us are not able to do so, at least not easily. Carrying with you the weight or burden of guilt from the past and not letting go of it but choosing to relive it again and again will impede the soul's spiritual progress to the Light and Joy of the Divine. If you are ready and willing to forgive others, including yourself, and acknowledge past grievances, hurt and regrets as illusions, you set yourself free, as only Love is real. Therefore, "Beyond a wholesome self-discipline, be gentle with yourself" (*Desiderata* verse 15).

Scriptural References

Buddhism

If anyone should give you a blow with their hand, with a stick, or with a knife, you should abandon any retaliatory desires.

(Majjhima Nikaya chapter 21 verse 16)

Christianity

If anyone strikes you on the cheek, offer the other also.

(Luke chapter 6 verse 29)

Forgive and you shall be forgiven.

(Luke chapter 6 verse 37)

Blessed are the merciful: for they shall obtain mercy.

(Matthew chapter 5 verse 7)

Forgive us our sins as we forgive those who trespass against us...For if you forgive the trespasses of others, your heavenly Father will also forgive you.

(Matthew chapter 6 verses 12 and 14)

When you stand praying, forgive, if you have anything against anyone: that your heavenly Father also may forgive your trespasses. But if you do not forgive, neither will your heavenly Father forgive your trespasses.

(Mark chapter 11 verses 25-6)

Be kind one to another, tender-hearted, forgiving one another, even as God for Christ's sake has forgiven you.

(Ephesians chapter 4 verse 32)

Forgive one another. If you have a quarrel with another: just as Christ forgave you, so also must you forgive.

(Colossians 3:13)

Confucianism

To be wronged is nothing unless you continue to remember it.

(Confucius)

Hinduism

Forgiveness.

(Saintly Virtue No. 22 of those endowed with a Divine Nature: Bhagavad-Gita chapter 16 verses 1-3)

Islam

Allah is al-'Afuw, the Pardoner, ever ready to forgive His servants.

(The Heights (or The Wall with Elevations) chapter 7 verse 180; Muhammad al-Madani, The Ninety-Nine Most Beautiful Names of Allah, No. 46)

A kind word and forgiveness are better than a charitable deed followed by insult.

(The Cow chapter 2 verse 263)

God loves those who pardon others.

(The Family of Imran chapter 3 verse 134)

Seek the forgiveness of God Who is forgiving and merciful.

(The Women chapter 4 verse 106)

If anyone forgoes retaliation by way of charity, it will serve for them as an atonement for their wrongdoing.

(The Table chapter 5 verse 45)

Show tolerance and forgiveness and enjoin what is good.

(The Heights (or The Wall with Elevations) chapter 7 verse 199)

God accepts repentance from His servants...God is always ready to accept repentance.

(The Repentance chapter 9 verse 104)

Your Lord is most forgiving and merciful.

(The Cave chapter 18 verse 58)

Despair not of the mercy of God; verily, God forgives all sins. He is most forgiving and merciful.

(The Troops chapter 39 verse 53)

Whoever forgives and makes reconciliation, their reward is with God.

(The Counsel chapter 42 verse 40)

Judaism

The Lord my God is gracious and merciful and He will not turn away His face from me if I return (confess my sins and ask for forgiveness) to Him.

(2 Chronicles chapter 30 verse 9)

Let the...unrighteous...return unto the Lord and He will have mercy upon them...He will abundantly pardon.

(Isaiah chapter 55 verses 6-7)

The merciful do good to their own soul.

(Proverbs chapter 11 verse 17)

They who have mercy on the poor, happy are they.

(Proverbs chapter 14 verse 21)

It is (a soul's) glory to pass over (forgive or overlook) a transgression.

(Proverbs chapter 19 verse 11)

Sikhism

They alone are truly truthful (righteous) who show mercy towards the living.

(Truth as the Heart of Conduct)

Love mercy and forbearance.

(From the Akal Ustat: Praise of the Immortal)

Zen Buddhism

When you forgive, you heal. When you let go, you grow.

(Zen proverb)

Chapter 17

Fortitude (Steadfastness in Faith/Spiritual Knowledge)

That which is "well planted is not easily uprooted; that which is well guarded is not easily taken away" (Lao Tzu, Tao Te Ching).

Fortitude is inner moral strength of spirit and conviction or depth of character, patient courage and endurance under affliction. It involves determination in the pursuit of spiritual elevation, even (or especially) in the face of adverse circumstances; persistence when hope appears unwarranted. Steadfastness comprises a firmly established, disciplined and unswerving faith, evidenced by constancy and lack of fickleness.

As it has been said, that which does not kill us makes us stronger. Although life's trials and tribulations may test our faith from time to time (and many trials are sent our way for that very purpose), they cultivate fortitude within us and it is important to remain steadfast and true to one's core set of spiritual beliefs and principles when being tested; undeterred by hardships, disappointments, distractions, diversions and temptations. A solid foundation or firm planting and nurturing of the seed in relation to one's faith will prevent compromise of, and deflection from, one's fundamental spiritual values and beliefs.

Scriptural References

Buddhism

By endeavour, diligence, discipline and self-mastery, the wise may make for themselves an island that no flood can overwhelm.

(The Dhammapada chapter 2 (On Earnestness) verse 25)

Christianity

Whosoever hears my words and acts upon them, I will liken them unto the wise, who built their house upon a rock. And the rain descended and the floods came and the winds blew and beat upon that house; and it fell not: for it was founded upon a rock.

(Matthew chapter 7 verses 24-5)

Always pray and never give up.

(Luke chapter 18 verse 1)

Be strong in the Lord and in the power of His might.

(Ephesians chapter 6 verse 10)

Fight the good fight of faith, lay hold on eternal life.

(1 Timothy chapter 6 verse 12)

Endure hardness, as a good soldier of Jesus Christ.

(2 Timothy chapter 2 verse 3)

Whenever you have to face trials of many kinds, consider yourself supremely happy, in the knowledge that such testing of your faith breeds fortitude.

(James chapter 1 verses 2-3)

Happy are they who remain steadfast under trial, for having passed that test they will receive for their prize the gift of life promised to those who love God.

(James chapter 1 verse 12)

Set your mind and keep it set on what is above (the matters of the spirit and the Hereafter), not on the things that are on (and of) the earth (worldly matters).

(Colossians chapter 3 verse 2)

I am firm (strong and determined) in faith.

(1 Peter chapter 5 verse 9)

Confucianism

Our greatest glory is not in ever falling, but in rising every time we fall.

(Confucius)

Desiderata

Nurture strength of spirit to shield you in sudden misfortune.

(Verse 12)

Hinduism

Steadfastness in spiritual knowledge.

(Saintly Virtue No. 3 of those endowed with a Divine Nature: Bhagavad-Gita chapter 16 verses 1-3)

Lack of fickleness.

(Saintly Virtue No. 20 of those endowed with a Divine Nature: Bhagavad-Gita chapter 16 verses 1-3)

Steadfast in their vows, doers of what is good and pure love and worship God.

(Bhakti and the Availability of God: Bhagavad-Gita chapter 7)

Great souls resort to Me (God), to Divine nature. Thinking of no one else, they worship Me...Making My name great as always, firm, not straying from their vow, revering Me in their devotion, constant in discipline, in reverence they know Me.

(Everything is a Sacrifice to Me: Bhagavad-Gita chapter 9)

Islam

The righteous are those who are steadfast in prayer and in times of misfortune and adversity.

(The Cow chapter 2 verse 177)

God is watching His servants, those who...are steadfast, sincere, obedient and charitable.

(The Family of Imran chapter 3 verse 17)

If you are steadfast and mindful of God, this is the best course.

(The Family of Imran chapter 3 verse 186)

The servants of the Merciful God...will be rewarded for their steadfastness with the highest abode in Paradise.

(The Discrimination chapter 25 verse 75)

Verily, along with every hardship is relief.

(The Opening Forth chapter 94 verse 5)

Jainism

The pious show an island to the beings which are carried away by the flood of the Samsara and suffer for their deeds.

(Sutrakrtanga: Book 1 Eleventh Lecture: The Path)

The Buddhas that were and the Buddhas that will be, they have Peace as their foundation...And if any accidents whatever befall those who have gained that foundation, they will not be overpowered by them as a mountain by the storm.

(Sutrakrtanga: Book 1 Eleventh Lecture: The Path)

Judaism

Those who wait upon the Lord shall renew their strength (patient endurance).

(Isaiah chapter 40 verse 31)

The righteous fall seven times and rise up again.

(Proverbs chapter 24 verse 16)

Taoism

Do not leave the roots (solid foundation of faith) to seek the branches.

(The Chieh Rules)

The thing that is well planted is not easily uprooted. The thing that is well guarded is not easily taken away.

(Lao Tzu, Tao Te Ching (To Cultivate Intuition) chapter 54)

Zoroastrianism

Without trouble nothing can be attained.

(The Vision of Arda-Viraf)

Chapter 18

Gentleness (Lenity)

Although the world may consider gentleness and sensitivity to others' feelings to be weaknesses, they are considered to be strengths and virtues in the Divine realms. To be gentle is to communicate or conduct oneself in a mild, tender, soft, kindly and careful manner which causes no harm to others. Gentleness of spirit and disposition or lenity (the quality of being mild or gentle as towards others) is a sign of spiritual refinement and, as such, is considered by some faiths to be a Divine Virtue. It is associated with a calm, peaceful and even temperament and demeanor, patience, avoidance of crude or inelegant behavior, sensitivity to others' feelings and a reluctance to pass judgment on others. Exhibiting gentleness to others defuses potential strife and inspires their respect, confidence and trust.

The manifestation of gentleness should extend not only to others (including all living beings) but to oneself, in the sense that although we should strive to maintain a healthy self-discipline and acknowledge and accept responsibility for our wrongdoings and errors of judgment, we must also not be too hard on ourselves. Be tender to yourself and do not judge yourself harshly (which many are prone to do). Gentleness is a prelude to peace (both internally within one's soul and externally in relations with others).

Know that as a child of God, you are deeply loved and cherished in Heaven; therefore accept yourself for who and what you are and do not judge yourself harshly, all the while striving to be the best possible version of your higher self.

Scriptural References

Baha'i

Verily, humanity is uplifted to the heaven of glory and power through meekness.

(Of Pride: Words of Wisdom from the Supreme Pen of Baha'u'llah)

Buddhism

Those who love the noble Dharma [Law], who are pure in word, thought and deed; always peaceful, gentle, focused and composed; they proceed through the world properly.

(Jatakamala chapter 3 verse 442)

Christianity

Blessed are the meek (gentle and submissive): for they shall inherit the earth.

(Matthew chapter 5 verse 5)

Take my yoke upon you and learn from me; for I am meek and lowly in heart (humble): and you shall find rest unto your souls.

(Matthew chapter 11 verse 29)

Be gentle and forbearing (having patient endurance) with others.

(Colossians chapter 3 verse 13)

Walk...with all lowliness and meekness...forbearing one another in love.

(Ephesians chapter 4 verses 1-2)

The servant of the Lord must...be gentle and patient unto all.

(2 Timothy chapter 2 verse 24)

Confucianism

Gentleness.

(One of five Confucian Virtues)

Desiderata
Beyond a wholesome discipline, be gentle with yourself.

(Verse 15)

Hinduism
Gentleness.

(Saintly Virtue No. 18 of those endowed with a Divine Nature: Bhagavad-Gita chapter 16 verses 1-3)

Islam
God loves gentleness in all affairs.

(Sahih al-Bukhari 6395)

By the Mercy of God, you (Prophet Muhammad) dealt with them gently.

(The Family of Imran chapter 3 verse 159)

The servants of the Merciful God are those who...walk upon the earth humbly and when the ignorant and aggressive address them (with bad words) they reply back with mild words of peace.

(The Discrimination chapter 25 verse 63)

Jainism
One should always be meek.

(Uttaradhyayana: First Lecture: On Discipline)

Judaism
A soft (gentle) answer turns away wrath: but grievous words stir up anger.

(Proverbs chapter 15 verse 1)

Taoism
Look to simplicity (gentleness, quietude and innocence); embrace purity; reduce one's possessions; diminish desire.

(Lao Tzu, Tao Te Ching (Return to Simplicity) chapter 19)

The tender and yielding conquer the rigid and strong (the spirit is stronger than flesh/matter).

(Lao Tzu, Tao Te Ching (Explanation of a Paradox) chapter 36)

In the world nothing is more fragile than water and yet of all the agencies that attack hard substances nothing can surpass it.

(Lao Tzu, Tao Te Ching (Trust and Faith) chapter 78)

Zen Buddhism

Only when you can be extremely pliable and soft can you be extremely hard and strong.

(Zen proverb)

Breathe gently through difficult moments: they will pass.

(Zen proverb)

Zoroastrianism

Among accusers be submissive, mild and kindly regardful.

(Commandments for the Body and the Soul)

Chapter 19

The Golden Rule (Reciprocity or Mutuality)

"Do unto others as you would have them do unto you" (New Testament: Luke chapter 6 verse 31). Or, to put it another way, never do to, or impose on, others what you would not desire or be prepared to do for yourself; treat others as you would wish to be treated.

This short, pithy maxim or principle of conduct has a potentially profound impact on our relations with others and represents a fundamental tenet of many faiths and belief systems. There are few other ethical exhortations which so forcefully and succinctly represent the essence of Divine Law and the source or parent of so many other Divine Virtues or Universal Ethical Principles.

From a Confucian perspective, the principle of reciprocity or mutuality constitutes the essence of propriety (the conventional standard of proper behavior) or proper conduct in society, while from a Western perspective, the Golden Rule postulates a mutual exchange of respect, care, toleration and deference (respectful or courteous regard). From a Buddhist perspective, the principle is essentially non-dualistic in eliminating the distinction between self and others (or, to put it another way, emphasizing the connectivity between us all). When internalized and actualized by the believer in daily social intercourse, it may be considered a Divine Virtue. Some faiths, such as Jainism, extend the Golden Rule's operation to encompass the treatment of all sentient or living beings by humanity.

Scriptural References

Baha'i

Courtesy is the lord of all the virtues.

(Tablet of the World: Baha'u'llah)

Buddhism

All tremble at punishment, all fear death; remember you are like unto them, so do not kill, nor cause slaughter [As life is dear to oneself, it is dear also to other living beings: by comparing oneself with others, good people bestow pity on all beings].

(The Dhammapada chapter 10 (Punishment) verse 129)

Christianity

Do unto others as you would have them do unto you.

(Luke chapter 6 verse 31)

Truly I tell you, whatever you did for one of the least of these brothers and sisters of mine, you did for me.

(Matthew chapter 25 verse 40)

Honour (respect) all you encounter.

(1 Peter chapter 2 verse 17)

Confucianism

Deference.

(One of five Confucian Virtues)

The feeling of respect is the beginning of propriety.

(The Innateness of the Four Great Virtues: Mencius)

Tzu-kung asked: Is there one word which can express the essence of right conduct in life? Confucius replied: "It is the word *shu* – reciprocity: Do not do to others what you do not want them to do to you."

(Analects)

Jainism

This is the quintessence of wisdom: not to kill anything. Know this to be the legitimate conclusion from the principle of the reciprocity with regard to non-killing.

(Sutrakrtanga: Book 1 Eleventh Lecture: The Path)

Indifferent to worldly objects, humanity should wander about treating all creatures (sentient beings) in the world as they themselves would wish to be treated.

(Sutrakrtanga: Book 1 Eleventh Lecture: The Path)

Judaism

You shall not...bear any grudge against (others), but you shall love your neighbor as yourself.

(Leviticus chapter 19 verse 18)

Taoism

Those who seek immortality must...treat others as they treat themselves.

(The Reward for Deeds: p'ao-p'u Tzu)

The Ten (Native American) Indian Commandments

Show great respect for your fellow human beings.

(Commandment No. 3)

Chapter 20

Humility (Absence of Pride and Vanity)

Self-centeredness and egotism separate humans from the Divine and prevent us from experiencing a greater communion with eternal spiritual truths. A common and recurring theme of the Abrahamic religions and Taoist scripture is that Heaven humbles those who exalt themselves and lifts up and honors the meek and the humble. Whereas pride brings shame and a fall from grace, wisdom dwells within those of a humble heart.

Humility is the quality of being humble; having a modest, as opposed to exaggerated, sense of one's own significance or worth (indeed, even viewing oneself as less than others and insignificant in the vast scheme of things – a form of enlightenment or awakening). Humility is regarding others before yourself. It is an absence of those qualities which may lead to contention, strife, discord and shame: namely, pride, arrogancy, haughtiness, vanity and self-absorption and self-focus. Some faiths consider pride to be a deadly sin and a defilement of the soul. Humility is the antithesis of boastfulness, self-praise, self-glorification, vainglory and self-aggrandizement. If a person affects to be great, for how long can they conceal their mediocrity? (Lao Tzu, Tao Te Ching).

Humility is rather being polite, courteous, modest, measured, respectful and submissive (perhaps even self-effacing); suppressing the ego and acknowledging, taking responsibility for, and growing and learning from, one's inevitable mistakes (that is to say, being refined and purified by life's trials). Humility also comprises selflessness, an appreciation of the finer qualities of others and gratitude to God for the finer qualities He has blessed us with.

Scriptural References

Baha'i

Be humble. Be servants of each other and know that we are less than anyone else.

(The Commands of the Blessed Master Abdul-Baha)

Divest yourselves from the garment of pride; and lay aside the robe of haughtiness...through pride is humanity degraded to the lowest station.

(Of Pride: Words of Wisdom from the Supreme Pen of Baha'u'llah)

Do you know why We have created you from one clay? That no one should glorify themselves over the other.

(Of the Light: Words of Wisdom from the Supreme Pen of Baha'u'llah)

Buddhism

One is the road that leads to (worldly) wealth, another road that leads to Nirvana; knowing this fact, the disciples of Buddha will not yearn for honour (glory), but will strive for separation from the world.

(The Dhammapada chapter 5 (The Fool) verse 75)

Christianity

Blessed are the meek (gentle and humble of spirit): for they shall inherit the earth.

(Matthew chapter 5 verse 5)

Whosoever...shall humble themselves as this little child, they shall be greatest in the Kingdom of Heaven.

(Matthew chapter 18 verse 4)

Many who are first (in this world) shall be last (in the Hereafter); and the last shall be first.

(Matthew chapter 19 verse 30)

They who exalt themselves shall be abased; and they who

humble themselves shall be exalted.

(Luke chapter 14 verse 11)

Let nothing be done through strife or vain-glory; but in lowliness of mind (humility) let each esteem the other better than themselves.

(Philippians chapter 2 verse 3)

Humble yourselves in the sight of the Lord and He shall lift you up.

(James chapter 4 verse 10)

Desiderata

If you compare yourself with others you may become vain and bitter, for always there will be greater and lesser persons than yourself.

(Verse 4)

Gandhi

So long as a person does not of their own free will put themselves last among their fellow creatures, there is no salvation for them. Ahimsa (non-violence) is the farthest limit of humility.

(Mohandas Gandhi, *An Autobiography*)

Hinduism

Absence of vanity.

(Saintly Virtue No. 26 of those endowed with a Divine Nature: Bhagavad-Gita chapter 16 verses 1-3)

Islam

Pray to your Lord with humility and in secret.

(The Heights (or The Wall with Elevations) chapter 7 verse 55)

Be not like those who come out of their homes with conceit and to be seen by others.

(The Spoils chapter 8 verse 47)

Those who believe and do what is right and humble

themselves before their Lord, they will be the dwellers of Paradise.

((Prophet) Hud chapter 11 verse 23)

Those who deny the life to come have faithless hearts and are puffed up with pride. God does not love the proud.

(The Bee chapter 16 verses 22-3)

Walk not in the earth proudly; you cannot break the earth open, nor match the mountains in height.

(The Journey by Night chapter 17 verse 37)

The servants of the Merciful God are those who walk upon the earth humbly.

(The Discrimination chapter 25 verse 63)

Twist not your cheek proudly, nor walk haughtily on the earth: God does not love the arrogant boaster. Rather let your stride be modest and your voice low.

(Loqman chapter 31 verses 18-19)

God is al-Khafid, the Humbler, Who humbles some while He exalts others.

(The Heights (or The Wall with Elevations) chapter 7 verse 180; Muhammad al-Madani The Ninety-Nine Most Beautiful Names of Allah No. 25)

Jainism

Pride is a passion which defiles the soul.

(Sutrakrtanga: Book 1 Sixth Lecture: Praise of Mahavira)

The wise and the pious combat various kinds of pride.

(Sutrakrtanga: Book 1 Thirteenth Lecture: The Real Truth)

Subdue your Self (ego), for the Self is difficult to subdue; if your Self is subdued, you will be happy in this world and in the next.

(Uttaradhyayana: First Lecture: On Discipline)

Liberation is attained by conquering the will.

(Uttaradhyayana: Fourth Lecture: Impurity)

Judaism

What does the Lord require of me? To act justly (with righteousness) and to love mercy and to walk humbly with my God.

(Micah chapter 6 verse 8)

The Lord leads the humble in what is right and the humble He teaches His way.

(Psalms chapter 25 verse 9)

The Lord lifts up the humble and downtrodden.

(Psalms chapter 147 verse 6)

The fear of the Lord (To be mindful of God) is to hate evil, pride and arrogancy.

(Proverbs chapter 8 verse 13)

When pride comes, then comes shame: but with the lowly (humble) is wisdom.

(Proverbs chapter 11 verse 2)

Pride brings contention.

(Proverbs chapter 13 verse 10)

Before honour is humility.

(Proverbs chapter 15 verse 33)

Pride precedes destruction and a haughty spirit precedes a fall.

(Proverbs chapter 16 verse 18)

Better it is to be of a humble spirit with the (meek and the poor) than to divide the spoil with the proud.

(Proverbs chapter 16 verse 19)

By humility and the fear of the Lord are riches (treasures of the heart) and honour and life.

(Proverbs chapter 22 verse 4)

Do not put yourself forth in the presence of the king and stand not in the place of great (individuals). For better it is that it is said to you, "Come up here"; then that you should be put lower.

(Proverbs chapter 25 verses 6-7)

To search your own glory is not glory.

(Proverbs chapter 25 verse 27)
They who have a proud heart stir up strife.
(Proverbs chapter 28 verse 25)
Pride shall bring a person low: but honour shall uphold the humble in spirit.
(Proverbs chapter 29 verse 23)
Favour is deceitful and beauty is vain.
(Proverbs chapter 31 verse 30)

Perfect Liberty Kyodan (modernized Shinto)
Our true self is revealed when our ego is effaced.
(Twenty-One Precepts No. 6)

Sikhism
Pride.
(One of five Sikh deadly sins)
O God, let our minds be for ever humble. O God, save us from the sin of egoism.
(The Community and its Past Saints: A Congregational Prayer)
May the minds of the Sikhs be humble but their intellects exalted!
(Sri Wahguru Ji Ki Fatah!)
Those whose hearts are full of love...are in bliss because they have no love of self. Only those that love God conquer love of self.
(Spiritual Marriage: The Bara Mah)
Those who understand God's commandments...are never guilty of egoism.
(God as Truth: Guru Nanak's Japji)
Those who know not the taste of God's essence bear the thorn of pride in their heart.
(From the Sohila: Guru Ram Das)
Those who are proud shall not be honoured on their arrival in the next world.

(Guru Nanak's Japji)

Taoism

Those who seek immortality must...not regard themselves highly, nor praise themselves.

(The Reward for Deeds: p'ao-p'u Tzu)

The best person is like water. Water is good; it benefits all things and does not compete with them. It dwells in lowly places that all disdain.

(Lao Tzu, Tao Te Ching (The Nature of Goodness) chapter 8)

The pride of wealth and position brings about their own misfortune.

(Lao Tzu, Tao Te Ching (Moderation) chapter 9)

Lessen the self (pride/ego).

(Lao Tzu, Tao Te Ching (Return to Simplicity) chapter 19)

The wise, not boasting of themselves, will acquire merit.

(Lao Tzu, Tao Te Ching (Increase by Humility) chapter 22)

Those who display themselves are not bright; those who assert themselves cannot shine. A self-approving person has no merit, nor does one who self-praises grow (spiritually evolve)... these things are detestable; Tao (the Way) does not dwell in them.

(Lao Tzu, Tao Te Ching (Troubles and Merit) chapter 24)

One should be resolute (firm or determined) but not boastful; resolute but not haughty; resolute but not arrogant.

(Lao Tzu, Tao Te Ching (Be Stingy of War) chapter 30)

They who practice Tao daily diminish. Again and again they humble themselves.

(Lao Tzu, Tao Te Ching (To Forget Knowledge) chapter 48)

To recognize one's insignificance (in the vast scheme of things) is called enlightenment...This is called practicing the eternal.

(Lao Tzu, Tao Te Ching (Return to Origin) chapter 52)

Tao has three treasures which one must guard and cherish...

the third is called humility...if one is humble they can become a useful servant.

(Lao Tzu, Tao Te Ching (Three Treasures) chapter 67)

If a person affects (purports or pretends) to be great, how long can they conceal their mediocrity?

(Lao Tzu, Tao Te Ching (Three Treasures) chapter 67)

The wise...accomplish merit, yet are not attached to it; neither do the wise (ostentatiously) display their excellence.

(Lao Tzu, Tao Te Ching (Tao of Heaven) chapter 77)

The mighty (the Tao of Heaven) humbles; the lowly it exalts. They who have abundance it diminishes and gives to them who have need...The human way is not so. Humans take from those who lack (the needy and underprivileged) to give to those who already abound (in material wealth and earthly fame).

(Lao Tzu, Tao Te Ching (Tao of Heaven) chapter 77)

Zen Buddhism

To forget the self (overcome the ego) is to be awakened by all things.

(Dogen)

Think lightly of yourself and deeply of the world (the nature of things).

(Miyamoto Musashi)

They who excel in employing (engaging) others humble themselves before them.

(Zen proverb)

Zoroastrianism

Be not haughty.

(Admonitions)

Those who are less than you consider as an equal and consider an equal as a superior.

(Commandments for the Body and the Soul)

Chapter 21

Living in the Present Moment (Contemplative Mindfulness)

Many of us are too busy contemplating and planning for the future or pondering over past mistakes and regrets to recognize and appreciate the beauty, wonder and awe of the present moment. Since we cannot change or undo our past and have only tenuous and limited control over the future, and acknowledging the impermanence of things, it is necessary to rejoice in the preciousness and fullness of the present moment. Maintaining a clear and focused mind, undistracted by regrets over our past and anxieties concerning the future, is a concept predominant within Buddhism, although it is also found in several Abrahamic religions. The Buddhist concept of right mindfulness is the ability to maintain constant and complete awareness of, or attentiveness to, what one is doing, thinking and feeling from moment to moment, unencumbered by past reflections and future apprehensions. One must fully, simply and calmly concentrate on the task at hand, completing each task one at a time. Our exclusive focus must be an awareness of the present moment (the 'Eternal Now'). This Divine Virtue therefore assists us in undertaking daily tasks wholeheartedly and vigorously rather than superficially and distractedly.

It has been said that the highest nobility lies in taming or stilling your own mind (Tibetan Buddhist Atisha). Mindfulness penetrates through to the reality underlying worldly appearances and delusions. Through mindfulness and meditation on Divine Virtues (a freeing of the mind), we awaken to the appreciation and joy of our existence. The universe is change; our life is what our thoughts make it (from *Meditations* by Roman Emperor Marcus Aurelius). Therefore, enjoy to the fullest each precious fleeting moment of this life; flow along with the river of life and accept with calm resignation whatever one cannot change.

Scriptural References

Buddhism

Do not pursue the past. Do not lose yourself in the future. The past no longer is. The future is yet to come. Looking very deeply at life as it is here and now, one dwells in stability and freedom.

(Bhaddekaratta Sutta)

All that we are is the result of what we have thought: it is founded on our thoughts, it is made up of our thoughts. If one acts or speaks with a pure thought, happiness follows them, like a shadow that never leaves.

(The Dhammapada chapter 1 (The Twin-Verses) verse 2)

The world does not know that we must all come to an end here; but those who know (and appreciate) it, their quarrels cease at once.

(The Dhammapada chapter 1 (The Twin-Verses) verse 6)

It is good to tame the mind, which is difficult to restrain and flighty, rushing wherever it lists. A tamed mind brings happiness.

(The Dhammapada chapter 3 (Thought) verse 35)

Give up what is before, give up what is behind, give up what is in the middle when you go to the other shore of existence. If your mind is altogether free, you will not again enter into birth and decay.

(The Dhammapada chapter 24 (Thirst) verse 348)

Do not dwell in the past. Do not dream of the future. Concentrate the mind on the present moment.

(The Buddha)

The resting place for the mind is in the heart.

(Anonymous Buddhist monk)

The secret of health for both mind and body is not to mourn

for the past, nor to worry about the future, but to live the present moment wisely and earnestly.

(Buddhist teaching)

Christianity

Take no thought (worry or anxiety) about what shall we eat or what shall we drink or what clothes shall we wear...But seek first the kingdom of God and His righteousness; and all these things shall be added unto you. Take therefore no thought for tomorrow, for tomorrow will have worries of its own. Sufficient for each day is its own trouble.

(Matthew chapter 6 verses 31, 33-4)

Confucianism

The mind is the master of the body.

(The Investigation of the Mind: Wang Yang-ming's Conversations with Huang I-fang)

Hinduism

Vigour.

(Saintly Virtue No. 21 of those endowed with a Divine Nature: Bhagavad-Gita chapter 16 verses 1-3)

Islam

Never say of anything, "I am going to do such and such thing tomorrow." Except (with the saying), "If God wills!"

(The Cave chapter 18 verses 23-4)

Judaism

As I think in my heart, so am I.

(Proverbs chapter 23 verse 7)

(Do not be too certain) of tomorrow; for you do not know what a day may bring forth.

(Proverbs chapter 27 verse 1)

Taoism

To the mind that is still, the whole universe surrenders.

(Lao Tzu)

Life is a series of natural and spontaneous changes. Don't resist them – that only creates sorrow. Let reality be reality. Let things flow naturally forward in whatever way they will.

(Lao Tzu)

We cannot see our reflection in running water. It is only in still water that we can see.

(Taoist proverb)

Zen Buddhism

Do one thing at a time. Do it slowly and deliberately. Do it completely.

(The Zen Manifesto)

Relearn everything. Let every moment be a new beginning.

(Zen proverb)

Be a master of the mind, not mastered by the mind.

(Zen proverb)

Zoroastrianism

Suffer no anxiety, for they who suffer from anxiety become less able to enjoy worldly and spiritual life and contraction happens to the body and soul.

(Commandments for the Body and the Soul)

Chapter 22

Loving-Kindness (Benevolence)

Conducting oneself with loving-kindness is to be kindly and lovingly disposed as opposed to being motivated by a malevolent heart. Loving-Kindness is an inner quality of the heart. It is an unconditional and loving desire (with no expectation of reciprocity) to do good to others which flows from spiritual love of the heart (in thought, word and deed); cultivating and exercising an overflowing warm and kind heart towards all living beings. As we spiritually grow to perceive the Divine love within us, that love is projected outwardly to those with whom we have contact.

The Divine Virtue of Loving-Kindness contains elements of mercy, compassion, charitableness, graciousness, benevolence, generosity of spirit, munificence (generosity in giving or bestowing), goodness and good-will and transcending self for the sake of the greater good of humanity. In its purest form, the Virtue involves an unconditional extension of unlimited and universal love, kindness, benevolent or deep affection and good-will to all living beings without discrimination. And do not forget to be kind to yourself. As God is Love and as God is Kindness, practicing Loving-Kindness in itself is a form of love for, worship of, and union with, God. There is nothing more important than aligning your thoughts, words and actions with Divine Love. Rain your kindness equally on all living beings, great and small (Buddhist teaching).

To extend unconditional love and acceptance to all living beings is the ultimate Reality and Truth and the basis of everything. All else is illusion. As we do not wish harm to befall us, let us not be the purveyors of harm to others. As we wish for good things to come our way, let us be the agents of goodness and kindness to others. Kind words uplift; kind deeds invoke love.

Scriptural References

Baha'i

To love each other fully. To be kind to all people and to love them with a pure spirit...All of our deeds must be done in kindness.

(The Commands of the Blessed Master Abdul-Baha)

O people of God! Be not occupied with yourselves. Be intent on the betterment of the world.

(Tablet of the World: Baha'u'llah)

The more we love each other, the nearer we shall be to God.

(The Commands of the Blessed Master Abdul-Baha)

Buddhism

Cultivate goodwill towards all beings. Let your thoughts of boundless love pervade the whole world.

(Sutta Nipata: Uragavagga, Mettasutta chapter 1.8.8 verse 149)

The Bhikshu (Buddhist monk) who acts with kindness will reach...the State of Calm (Peace and Contentment), the cessation of natural desires and happiness.

(The Dhammapada chapter 25 (The Bhikshu/Mendicant) verse 368)

As rain falls equally on the just and unjust, do not burden your heart with judgments but rain your kindness equally on all.

(Buddhist teaching)

Christianity

A new commandment I give unto you, that you love one another; as I have loved you, that you also love one another.

(John chapter 13 verse 34)

Greater love has no one than this, to lay down one's life for a friend.

(John chapter 15 verse 13)

You shall love the Lord your God with all your heart and with all your soul and with all your strength and with all your mind; and your neighbor (others) as yourself.

(Luke chapter 10 verse 27)

Love your enemy.

(Matthew chapter 5 verse 44)

If you (only) love those who love you, what reward have you? Do not even the publicans (tax collectors) do the same? And if you salute your (kin) only, what do you have more than others? Do not the publicans do so?

(Matthew chapter 5 verses 46-7)

Love...is kind.

(1 Corinthians chapter 13 verse 4)

Let us love one another: for love is of God: and every one who loves is born of God and knows God. Whosoever loves not knows not God: for God is love.

(1 John chapter 4 verses 7-8)

Confucianism

Identify oneself with the welfare of the whole body (community).

(The Well-Ordered Society: Doctrine of the Mean)

Desiderata

As far as possible be on good terms with all persons.

(Verse 2)

Islam

A good (kind) word is like a good tree, whose root is firm and its branches reach the sky...giving its fruit at every season.

((Prophet) Abraham chapter 14 verses 24-5)

Allah is al-Halim, the Kindly, who is both forgiving and kindly disposed...Allah is al-Karim, the Munificent (generous in bestowing), who is...generous.

(The Heights (or The Wall with Elevations) chapter 7 verse 180; Muhammad al-Madani The Ninety-Nine Most Beautiful Names of Allah No. 21 and No. 60 respectively)

Judaism

Thus speaks the Lord of hosts, saying, "Execute true judgment, and show mercy and compassion to all."

(Zechariah chapter 7 verse 9)

The Lord is merciful and gracious (kind/benevolent), slow to anger and plenteous in mercy.

(Psalms chapter 103 verse 8)

The highest wisdom is loving-kindness.

(The Babylonian Talmud: Berakhot, 17A)

Shintoism

Extend your benevolence to all...advance public good and promote common interests.

(The Japanese Ethos: Imperial Rescript on Education 30 October 1890 (modernized Shinto))

Sikhism

Do good to the world.

(Nanak's Call: A Janamsakhi)

Taoism

Those who seek immortality must...be kind to all things.

(The Reward for Deeds: p'ao-p'u Tzu)

Those who aspire to practice the virtue of benevolence will find contentment, peace and rest.

(Lao Tzu, Tao Te Ching (The Virtue (*Teh*) of Benevolence) chapter 35)

Superior benevolence...does not become pretentious (it remains authentic and without selfish motives)...The great (soul) conforms to the spirit and not to external appearance. It goes on to fruitage and does not rest in the show of blossom. It...practices true benevolence.

(Lao Tzu, Tao Te Ching (A Discussion About *Teh* (Virtue)) chapter 38)

With beautiful words one may sell goods but in winning people one can accomplish more by kindness.

(Lao Tzu, Tao Te Ching (The Practice of Tao) chapter 62)

The Ten (Native American) Indian Commandments

Dedicate a share of your efforts to the greater good.

(Commandment No. 8)

Zen Buddhism

One kind word can warm three winter months.

(Japanese proverb)

Chapter 23

Natural Environment (Respect and Reverence for)

Those faiths which accept that God is omnipresent (present everywhere and in all things) and the transcendent reality of which the material world is but a manifestation, must accept as a corollary the identification of God with, and in, Nature (or Mother Earth) as creator, sustainer, protector and benevolent provider to all sentient beings. Our spiritual perception must be refined such that we observe God not only in other human beings but in all sentient beings and in Nature itself. Sikhism stresses the need to perceive the Divine in the created world including Nature. Certain Eastern faiths such as Shintoism and various indigenous belief systems believe that everything – all life and natural phenomena and the forces thereof – is imbued with spirit and consciousness, containing aspects of both animism and pantheism. According to Taoism, the actions and processes of Nature are manifestations of the Tao which must be emulated in human life. Reverence for God must therefore extend to love and respect for the flora and fauna of this our most beautiful planet (an ecological faith, as it were), as well as thanksgiving for the Earth's abundant provision.

An element of stewardship or guardianship by humanity over Nature is involved, whereby one should act in a manner that is harmonious with Nature rather than act exclusively for the benefit of oneself (Taoism), such that one should not take therefrom more than one's basic needs require (Native American Indian belief and practice). The natural environment provides life, sustenance and nurture; connection and context; foundation and orientation. One should therefore work with Nature, not against it; all the while appreciating Nature's seasons, just as there is a season for everything during one's life journey.

This Divine Virtue is captured well by the essential harmony and intimacy between God, divine spirits, Nature and humanity which underlies the world-view of Shintoism, that is to say, the interdependence of all spiritual and material life and existence. After having for too long a period subjugated and exploited Nature and its resources, borne of greed and selfish motives, humanity must now reawaken to its sacred duty or trust as steward/guardian to address the pressing need to reestablish the pristine balance and harmony between humanity and Nature.

Scriptural References

Buddhism
Earth brings us to life and nourishes us. Earth takes us back again. Birth and death are present in every breath.

(Thich Nhat Hahn's Gathas)

Obey the nature of things and you will walk freely and undisturbed.

(Sengcan)

Hinduism
The God who is in fire, who is in water, who has entered the whole world, who is in plants, who is in trees – to that God be adoration!

(Svetasvatara Upanisad chapter 2 verses 8-17)

I am omnipresent...All beings exist in me...All creatures enter into my nature...I appear as an onlooker, detached... Nature gives birth to all moving and unmoving things. I supervise. That is how the world keeps turning.

(Everything is a Sacrifice to Me: Bhagavad-Gita chapter 9)

Islam
Verily, it is God Who causes the seed grain and the fruit stone to

split and sprout. He brings forth the living from the dead.

(The Cattle chapter 6 verse 95)

To God belongs the kingdom of the heavens and the earth. He gives life and He causes death.

(The Repentance chapter 9 verse 116)

No creature that walks upon the earth is there but its provision is from God. And He knows its dwelling-place.

((Prophet) Hud chapter 11 verse 6)

God is the Guardian over all things.

((Prophet) Hud chapter 11 verse 12)

It is God who sends down water from the sky, which provides you with your drink and brings forth the pasturage on which your cattle feed. And with it He brings forth corn and olives, dates and grapes and fruits of every kind. Surely in this there is a sign for those who think. He has pressed the night and the day and the sun and the moon into your service: the stars also serve you by His leave. Surely in this there is a sign for the prudent. It is He who has subdued the ocean, so that you may eat of its fresh flesh...All this, that you may seek His bounty and render thanks. He set firm mountains upon the earth and rivers...so that you may be rightly guided.

(The Bee chapter 16 verses 10-16)

God has made from water every living thing.

(The Prophets chapter 21 verse 30)

When you see the parched earth, God sends down water (rain) on it and it stirs and swells and brings forth herbs of every beauteous kind.

(The Pilgrimage chapter 22 verse 5)

God sends the winds as heralds of glad tidings, going before His mercy (rain); and We send down pure water from the heavens, that We may give life thereby to a dead land and We give to drink thereof the cattle and (humanity) that We have created.

(The Discrimination chapter 25 verses 48-9)

God has spread the earth out and set thereon mountains standing firm and has produced therein every kind of lovely growth (plants)...And God sends down blessed water from the heaven, then God produces therewith gardens and grain (and every kind of harvest) that are reaped...God gives life therewith to a dead land.

(Qaf chapter 50 verses 7, 9 and 11)

God has made the earth manageable for you, so...eat of His provision.

(The Kingdom chapter 67 verse 15)

Judaism

God said, "Let us make man in our image, after our likeness: and let (humanity) have dominion (stewardship) over the fish of the sea and over the foul of the air and over the cattle and over all the Earth."

(Genesis chapter 1 verse 26)

In wisdom have You (God) made them all; the earth is full of your creatures...These all look to You to give them food in due season...when You open Your hand, they are filled with good things (God as the benevolent provider).

(Psalms chapter 104 verses 24, 27-8)

Shintoism

Let not humanity subjugate Nature; rather, let humanity be its prudent steward.

(A Coalescent Harmony between Humankind and Nature: Kokutai no Hongi)

Love nature.

(A Coalescent Harmony between Humankind and Nature: Kokutai no Hongi)

Sikhism

Thou (God) art in the tree, Thou art in its leaves. Thou art in the earth.

(Sikh doctrine on the pantheistic conception of God from the Akal Ustat: Praise of the Immortal)

He (God) who created things of different colours, descriptions and species, beholdeth His handiwork which attests to His greatness.

(Guru Nanak's Japji)

Trees, the banks of sacred streams, clouds, fields, islands, peoples...continents...lakes, mountains, animals – O Nanak, God knoweth their condition. Nanak, God having created animals taketh care of them all.

(Guru Nanak)

Taoism

Follow the nature of things (Nature's processes and phenomena).

(The Domain of Nothingness: Chuang Tzu)

(Humanity) is derived from nature, nature is derived from Heaven. Heaven is derived from Tao. Tao is self-derived (self-subsistent).

(Lao Tzu, Tao Te Ching (Describing the Mysterious) chapter 25)

The Ten (Native American) Indian Commandments

Treat the (Mother) Earth and all (living sentient beings) that dwell thereon with respect.

(Commandment No. 1)

Zen Buddhism

Find beauty in imperfection, accept the natural cycle of growth and decay (and regrowth).

(Zen proverb)

Zoroastrianism

I (Ahura-Mazda/God) have made every land dear to its dwellers, even though it had no charms whatever in it.

(The Creation of the World by Ahura-Mazda)

They who till the earth...unto them will the earth bring forth plenty...They who sow corn sow holiness: they make the Law of Ahura-Mazda grow higher and higher.

(Blessings of Cultivating the Soil)

Chapter 24

Non-Judgmental Disposition
(Absence of Fault-Finding)

We judge others and they judge us; we even judge and condemn ourselves on what we have done or not yet achieved, verily virtually on a daily basis. As we observed in Chapter 7, God is omnipresent and immanent: there is no place that God is not, including within all of His creatures. We must therefore love, respect and honor others as well as ourselves (while staying clear of pride and excessive ego). Fault-finding is perhaps one of the most intractable of human foibles. Often we do so without sufficient facts, information, context and empathy. But such judgment is of the human domain; in the Divine realms such judgment is antithetical to the unconditional Love and Compassion of a Merciful God.

The human propensity to identify and criticize the faults and shortcomings of others clouds and pollutes the mind. If we judge others, we risk being judged ourselves in turn, indeed by the very standard we use to cast judgment on others. If we wish to avoid being judged, it is necessary to exercise restraint in finding fault with, and judging, others. We must perceive in all people a portion of God's spirit and acknowledge that they are His precious creation. Remember that when you observe others in judgment, God – Love – is within their soul too. But if you cannot escape the deeply engrained propensity to judge, at least do so with fairness (Qur'an chapter 4 verse 58) and seek to kindly assist the person to overcome their faults (Baha'i). Nevertheless, perhaps we should not cast the first stone if we ourselves are blemished (New Testament: John chapter 8 verse 7).

A more positive approach, and one which purifies the mind, is to identify and appreciate the finer qualities and virtues in others, all the while examining our own lives to assess the extent to which we have fallen short of the glory of God. See the best and the Divine in others. Search for goodness in others and you will find it; become what you respect and admire. Reflecting on and addressing our own flaws and defects while admiring the positive character traits of others, elevates us spiritually and moves us away from a closed, intolerant and biased mind towards an open, tolerant and impartial mind. Only a closed mind is certain; an open mind is receptive to enlightenment. "A tree that is unbending is easily broken" (Lao Tzu); a tree which is flexible and supple grows to maturity.

The great teachers like Jesus Christ and the Buddha taught, and associated with, all social classes and types of people, applying the principle of non-distinction. Clinging to the ego-oriented notion of self arouses passions which defile the soul; by no longer distinguishing between self and others, we appreciate their essential and inherent interconnectedness and unity.

Scriptural References

Baha'i

Why have you overlooked your own faults and are observing defects in My servants? Whosoever does this is condemned by Me. Breathe not the sins of any one as long as you are a sinner. If you do contrary to this command, you are not of Me. To this I bear witness.

(On Disputation and Fault-Finding: Words of Wisdom from the Supreme Pen of Baha'u'llah)

To be silent concerning the faults of others; to pray for them; and help them, through kindness, to correct their faults. To look always at the good and not at the bad...To never allow ourselves to speak one unkind word about another; even though that other be our enemy. To rebuke those who speak to us of the faults of others.

(The Commands of the Blessed Master Abdul-Baha)

Think not the faults of others to be great, that your own may not seem great.

(On Disputation and Fault-Finding: Words of Wisdom from the Supreme Pen of Baha'u'llah)

Buddhism

The faults of others are easier to see than one's own.

(Udanavarga chapter 27 verse 1)

One should not dwell on the faults of others, into things done and left undone by others. One should rather consider what by oneself is done and left undone.

(The Dhammapada chapter 4 (Flowers) verse 50)

Those who understand both sides in this world are called a sage.

(The Dhammapada chapter 19 (The Just) verse 219)

Christianity

Those who are without sin, let them cast the first stone.

(John chapter 8 verse 7)

Judge not and you shall not be judged: condemn not and you shall not be condemned.

(Luke chapter 6 verse 37)

Judge not, that you be not judged. For with what judgment you judge, you shall be judged: and with what measure you mete, it shall be measured to you again. And why do you behold the mote (speck) that is in your (neighbor's) eye, but consider not the beam that is in your own eye?

(Matthew chapter 7 verses 1-3)

Confucianism

The mind is the master of the body…Therefore to cultivate the personal life lies in realizing through personal experience the true substance of one's mind and always making it broad and extremely impartial.

(The Investigation of the Mind: Wang Yang-ming's Conversations with Huang I-fang)

Hinduism

Restraint from fault-finding.

(Saintly Virtue No. 15 of those endowed with a Divine Nature: Bhagavad-Gita chapter 16 verses 1-3)

By dualities are people confused and these arise from desire and hate.

(Bhakti and the Availability of God: Bhagavad-Gita chapter 7)

When a seer sees the brilliant Maker (Creator), Lord... everything is reduced to unity (interconnectedness).

(Maitri Upanisad chapter 6 verses 18-19)

Islam

God commands that if you judge between people, judge with fairness.

(The Women chapter 4 verse 58)

Jainism

Hearing the talk of people, one should not say, "This is a good action" nor "This is a bad action".

(Sutrakrtanga: Book 1 Eleventh Lecture: The Path)

Look at all people with an impartial mind.

(Sutrakrtanga: Book 1 Tenth Lecture: Carefulness)

One should be impartial like a sage.

(Uttaradhyayana: Fourth Lecture: Impurity)

Taoism

Distinctions (based, for example, on wealth, power and fame) vanish in the Tao (the Way) and after death.

(The Great and the Small: Chuang Tzu)

Complete harmony with the Tao means seeing the world

as it is without distinctions (essential and inherent unity or interconnectedness).

(The Domain of Nothingness: Chuang Tzu)

Identify yourself with non-distinction. Follow the nature of things and admit no personal bias, then the world will be in peace.

(The Domain of Nothingness: Chuang Tzu)

Seek to attain an open mind...comprehension (understanding) makes one broad-minded; breadth of vision brings nobility; nobility is like Heaven.

(Lao Tzu, Tao Te Ching (Returning to the Source) chapter 16)

All beings are on the path (of enlightenment), all victims of the same (earthly) existence...No one is better than the next person.

(Deng Ming-Dao)

Chapter 25

Non-Violence/Non-Injury
(Prohibition of Killing)

All life, in whatever form, is sacred, having been bestowed by the Creator. The taking of such life, or harm, abuse, violence or torment to such life, is of the human, and not of the Divine, realm. The Divine Virtues of Compassion, Gentleness, the Golden Rule and Humility provide the basis of this Universal Ethical Principle which forbids the killing of, or violence against, others.

While confined in its operation to human beings in the Abrahamic religions, this Divine Virtue concerns respect and reverence for the life and well-being of all sentient beings (any living creature that breathes and feels/has the power of perception by the senses/contains the life-force) in thought, word and deed. Non-injury to all living beings (*Ahimsa*), including minute forms of life, is a central ethical tenet of Jainism, Buddhism, Hinduism and Taoism. It is an affirmation of the sanctity of life, the greatest gift of all, including one's own, such that one must avoid causing harm or life-damaging violence to persons and sentient beings, including oneself, by act or omission. One must be able to love the lowest of creation as oneself (Mohandas Gandhi, *An Autobiography*). From the 'Golden Rule' perspective, when you harm another living being, you also harm yourself and the whole.

Scriptural References

Buddhism
Abstain from killing.
   (Khuddakapatha 2)

Abstain from taking life. Do not kill anything that lives/has the life-force.

(First Basic Precept: The Five Precepts and their Meaning: Buddhagosa's Commentary: Papanasudani)

All tremble at punishment; all fear death. Remember that you are like them, therefore one should not kill, nor cause to slaughter.

(The Dhammapada chapter 10 (Punishment) verse 129)

Christianity

Those who live by the sword shall die by the sword.

(Matthew chapter 26 verse 52)

You shall not murder.

(Romans chapter 13 verse 9)

Gandhi

To see that universal and all-pervading Spirit of Truth (God) face to face, one must be able to love the meanest of creation as oneself.

(Mohandas Gandhi, *An Autobiography*)

Hinduism

Non-violence.

(Saintly Virtue No. 10 of those endowed with a Divine Nature: Bhagavad-Gita chapter 16 verses 1-3)

Islam

Do not kill yourselves.

(The Women chapter 4 verse 29)

If anyone killed a person not in retaliation of murder...it would be as if they killed all (humanity) and if anyone saved a life, it would be as if they saved the life of all (humanity).

(The Table chapter 5 verse 32)

You shall not take life – for that is forbidden by God – except for a just cause. Thus God exhorts you, that you may grow in wisdom.

(The Cattle chapter 6 verse 151)

Slay not your children [infanticide] for fear of poverty; We will provide for you and them; the slaying of them is a grievous sin.

(The Journey by Night chapter 17 verse 31)

You shall not kill the soul that God has forbidden you to kill, except for a just cause.

(The Journey by Night chapter 17 verse 33)

Jainism

I renounce all killing of living beings...Nor shall I myself kill living beings (nor cause others to do it, nor consent to it).

(First Great Vow: Acaranga Sutra)

Having heard (the eternal law) humans will...abstain from killing living beings.

(Uttaradhyayana: Third Lecture: The Four Requisites)

All breathing, existing, living, sentient creatures should not be slain, nor treated with violence, nor abused, nor tormented. This is the pure, unchangeable, eternal law.

(Acaranga Sutra: Fourth Lecture: Righteousness)

A monk who is possessed of carefulness should give no offence to any creature.

(Sutrakrtanga: Book 1 Tenth Lecture: Carefulness)

A true monk should not accept any food...involving the slaughter of living beings...this is the Law of those who are rich in control.

(Sutrakrtanga: Book 1 Eleventh Lecture: The Path)

Those who guard their soul and subdue their senses should never assent to anybody killing living beings.

(Sutrakrtanga: Book 1 Eleventh Lecture: The Path)

One should do no harm to anybody, neither by thoughts, nor words, nor acts.

(Sutrakrtanga: Book 1 Eleventh Lecture: The Path)

This is the quintessence of wisdom: not to kill anything...
One should cease to injure living beings...For this has been
called the Nirvana, which consists in peace.

(Sutrakrtanga: Book 1 Eleventh Lecture: The Path)

Judaism

You shall not kill.

(The Ten Commandments: Commandment No. 6 Exodus
chapter 20 verse 13 and Deuteronomy chapter 5 verse 17)

Taoism

Those who seek immortality must...extend their humaneness
(*jen*) (compassion)...even to insects...Their hands must never
injure life.

(The Reward for Deeds: p'ao-p'u Tzu)

The superior fighter succeeds without violence.

(Lao Tzu, Tao Te Ching (Compliance with Heaven) chapter 68)

The Ten (Native American) Indian Commandments

Show great respect for your fellow human beings.

(Commandment No. 3)

Wavoka's Letter

You must not hurt anybody or do harm to anyone.

(The Ghost Dance)

Zoroastrianism

Be not cruel...Torment not.

(Admonitions)

Chapter 26

Patience (Forbearance)

Impatience comes easily to humanity; patience is much harder to display, particularly in the face of unexpected provocation or an expectation which seems too long in materializing. Patience is quiet perseverance, calm and uncomplaining waiting or endurance and forbearance in the sense of refraining from. It also involves discretion and acceptance (of oneself and others as well as passing hardships). According to the adage, patience is a virtue and, according to the Holy Scriptures of numerous mainstream faiths, patience is also a Divine Virtue. As such, it has a dual aspect: trust in the wisdom of God's timing as a temporal reference-point rather than on human expectation of timing (we often misguidedly seek instant gratification in our prayer life) and exercising discipline, restraint or self-control in reacting to negative external stimuli.

Those who are patient substitute wisdom, forgiveness and intellect for raw emotion and understand the human psyche. Patience cultivates depth of character, spiritual refinement and understanding. Everything comes to us at the right moment (Zen proverb) and patience in an angry moment will obviate one hundred days of sorrow (Chinese proverb).

Scriptural References

Buddhism
The Enlightened call patience the highest penance.

(The Dhammapada chapter 14 (The Buddha/The Awakened) verse 184)

Christianity
By steadfastness and patient endurance I shall win my soul.

(Luke chapter 21 verse 19)

Tribulation (hardship and affliction) produces patience (endurance) and patience produces experience (maturity of character and wisdom).

(Romans chapter 5 verses 3-4)

For you have need of patience, that after you have done the will of God, you might receive the promise (of eternal life).

(Hebrews chapter 10 verse 36)

Be joyful when you fall into diverse temptations...as the testing of your faith produces patience.

(James chapter 1 verses 2-3)

Hinduism
Patiently bear hard (provocative) words, do not insult anybody.

(The Laws of Manu: Manava-dharma-sastra chapter 6 verses 33-60)

Islam
Believers, strengthen yourselves with patience and with prayer. Truly, God is with those who are patient.

(The Cow chapter 2 verse 153)

God loves the patient.

(The Family of Imran chapter 3 verse 146)

You shall certainly be tried and tested in your wealth and in your personal lives...but if you persevere patiently and become pious, you will surely triumph.

(The Family of Imran chapter 3 verse 186)

If one charitably forbears from retaliation, such remission shall atone for bad deeds.

(The Table chapter 5 verse 45)

God is...Most Forbearing.

(The Table chapter 5 verse 101)

Those who are patient and do righteous good deeds: theirs will be forgiveness and a great reward (Paradise).

((Prophet) Hud chapter 11 verse 11)

It shall be best for you to endure wrongs with patience. Be patient, then: God will grant you patience.

(The Bee chapter 16 verses 126-7)

God is Lord of the heavens and the earth and all that is between them. Worship Him, then, and be patient in His service.

(Mary chapter 19 verse 65)

Impatience is the very stuff humanity is made of. I will show you My signs; but do not hurry Me.

(The Prophets chapter 21 verse 37)

The servants of the Merciful God...shall be rewarded with the highest heaven (ascending heavens); for that they endured patiently.

(The Discrimination chapter 25 verse 75)

Bear with patience whatever befalls you.

(Loqman chapter 31 verse 17)

Repel evil with good and those who are your enemy will become your dearest friend. But none will attain goodness except those who patiently endure.

(They are explained in detail chapter 41 verses 34-5)

Whosoever shows patience and forgives, that is a duty to God incumbent on all.

(The Counsel chapter 42 verse 43)

Verily, humanity was created very impatient; irritable when evil touches them and niggardly when good touches them.

(The Ways of Ascent chapter 70 verses 19-21)

Jainism

Acquire fame (honour) through patience. You will rise to the upper regions (ascending heavens) after having left this body of clay.

(Uttaradhyayana: Third Lecture: The Four Requisites)

Judaism

But these things I plan won't happen right away. Slowly, steadily, surely, the time approaches when the vision will be fulfilled. If it seems slow, do not despair, for these things will surely come to pass. Just be patient! They will not be overdue a single day.

(Habakkuk chapter 2 verse 3)

Better is the end of a thing than the beginning of it and the patient in spirit is better than the proud in spirit.

(Ecclesiastes chapter 7 verse 8)

You are my God. My times are in Your hand.

(Psalms chapter 31 verses 14-15)

I won't be impatient for the Lord to act! I will keep traveling steadily along His pathway and in due season (God's time) He will honor me with every blessing.

(Psalms chapter 37 verse 34)

Those of quick temper act foolishly, but those of discretion are patient.

(Proverbs chapter 14 verse 17)

One who is slow to anger is of great understanding.

(Proverbs chapter 14 verse 29)

A soft (patient and gentle) answer turns away wrath; but grievous words stir up anger.

(Proverbs chapter 15 verse 1)

Sikhism

Patience.

(One of five Sikh Virtues)

Always practise mildness and patience.

(From the Akal-Ustat: Praise of the Immortal)

Righteousness is the offspring of mercy, which supported by patience maintains the order of nature.

(The Repetition of the Divine Name: The Japji)

Taoism

By patience the animal spirits (base human instincts) can be disciplined.

(Lao Tzu, Tao Te Ching (What is Possible) chapter 10)

One should avoid assertion and practice inaction (in the sense of not forcing things or imposing one's personal views).

(Lao Tzu, Tao Te Ching (A Consideration of Beginnings) chapter 63)

A tree that it takes both arms to encircle grew from a tiny rootlet...A journey of three thousand miles begins with one step.

(Lao Tzu, Tao Te Ching (Consider the Insignificant) chapter 64)

Zen Buddhism

Cultivate patience. Everything comes to you at the right moment.

(Zen proverb)

If you are patient in one moment of anger, you will escape a hundred days of sorrow.

(Chinese proverb)

Chapter 27

Peacefulness (Equanimity) and Contentment

Do not seek peacefulness without; it may only be found within (Zen proverb). Such peace is not of this world, but of the Divine. It transcends all understanding (New Testament: Philippians chapter 4 verse 7). False riches are perceived with the eye; true riches reside within the heart and soul.

Peacefulness is a state of mind; the ability to remain equipoised (retaining an inner equilibrium or even balance) in the face of disturbing external circumstances. Peacefulness may be described as inner peace and contentment; the tranquil state of a soul content with its earthly condition. While happiness and its causes are fleeting, contentment is more enduring, resting upon a more solid and spiritual foundation. Equanimity is the ability to navigate through life and all of its vicissitudes with a calm, mild, placid and composed mind (mental poise) without being disturbed.

From Buddhist and Hindu perspectives, the attainment of a peaceful, serene and mindful inner calm is secured by the letting go of cravings and desires and by becoming dispassionate (free from passions and emotions). Rejoice in what you have been blessed with; pine or grieve not for what you do not possess. From a Taoist perspective, the concept of *wu wei* encourages one to 'go with the flow' or to drift with the current of life rather than constantly and doggedly struggling against it. From an Abrahamic tradition, believers are encouraged to passively and graciously accept a surrender to the Will of God as the gateway to Heaven. Be comfortable with and accept yourself, your lot in life and others. Having let go of the past, not fretting over a future which has not yet come, rest content in the fullness of the present moment.

Apart from being at peace with and within oneself, such peacefulness may be externalized in the sense of striving to maintain peaceful relations with others to the greatest extent practicable and possible. Blessed are the peacemakers (New Testament: Matthew chapter 5 verse 9).

Scriptural References

Baha'i

Verily I say the most negligent of God's servants are they who dispute and prefer themselves to others.

(Of Disputation and Fault-Finding: Words of Wisdom from the Supreme Pen of Baha'u'llah)

Buddhism

Wise people, after they have listened to the [Teaching], become serene, like a deep, smooth and still lake.

(The Dhammapada chapter 6 (The Wise Man/Pandita) verse 82)

Calm is the thought, calm the word and deed of those who have obtained freedom by true knowledge, perfectly peaceful and equipoised.

(The Dhammapada chapter 7 (The Venerable/Arhat) verse 96)

The contented rest in happiness, giving up both victory and defeat.

(The Dhammapada chapter 15 (Happiness) verse 201)

Health is the greatest of gifts, contentedness the best riches.

(The Dhammapada chapter 15 (Happiness) verse 204)

Having tasted the sweetness of solitude and tranquillity, one becomes free from fear and sin.

(The Dhammapada chapter 15 (Happiness) verse 205)

Do not grieve over what is no more.

(The Dhammapada chapter 25 (The Bhikshu/Mendicant) verse 367)

Christianity

Blessed are the peacemakers: for they shall be called the children of God.

(Matthew chapter 5 verse 9)

Peace I leave with you; My peace I now give and bequeath to you. Not as the world gives do I give to you. Do not let your hearts be troubled, neither let them be afraid.

(John chapter 14 verse 27)

If it be possible, as much as lies within you, live peaceably with all.

(Romans chapter 12 verse 18)

Strive to live in peace with everybody and pursue that... holiness without which no one will see the Lord.

(Hebrews chapter 12 verse 14)

God's peace...transcends all understanding.

(Philippians chapter 4 verse 7)

Godliness with contentment (a treasure of the heart) is great gain, for we brought nothing (material) into the world, and we cannot take anything out of the world.

(1 Timothy chapter 6 verses 6-7)

Confucianism

With rough rice to eat and water to drink and one's bent arm to be a pillow, there is still happiness (contentment).

(Confucius' Conversation and Manners: Analects)

Einstein

From discord find harmony.

(Albert Einstein)

Hinduism

Those who desire happiness must strive after a perfectly contented disposition and for self-control...for happiness has contentment for its root.

(The Laws of Manu: Manava-dharma-sastra chapter 4 verses 1-18)

Peacefulness.

(Saintly Virtue No. 14 of those endowed with a Divine Nature: Bhagavad-Gita chapter 16 verses 1-3)

Islam

There is virtue in those who enjoin charity, kindness and reconciliation among humanity. Those who do this to please God, on them shall God bestow a rich reward.

(The Women chapter 4 verse 114)

The servants of God are those who walk on the earth humbly and sedately, and when the ignorant (rude and aggressive) address them reply back with mild and peaceful words.

(The Discrimination chapter 25 verse 63)

It was God who sent down calmness and tranquillity into the hearts of the believers, so that their faith might grow stronger.

(The Victory chapter 48 verse 4)

Do not grieve over things you fail to get.

(Iron chapter 57 verse 23)

Allah is al-Salam, the Peace-Maker, whose name is Peace.

(The Heights (or The Wall with Elevations) chapter 7 verse 180; Muhammad al-Madani The Ninety-Nine Most Beautiful Names of Allah No. 35)

Jainism

Have equanimity (calmness and mental poise) towards all.

(The Lay Person's Inner Voyage: Nityanaimittika-pathavali)

Whether it is life or death, whether gain or loss, whether defeat or victory, whether meeting or separation, whether friend or enemy, whether pleasure or pain, I have equanimity towards all.

(The Lay Person's Inner Voyage: Nityanaimittika-pathavali)

The wise should abstain from fights and quarrels.

(Sutrakrtanga: Book 1 Lecture 9: The Law)

If beaten, a monk should not be angry; if abused, he should not fly into a passion; with a placid mind he should bear everything and not make a great noise.

(Sutrakrtanga: Book 1 Lecture 9: The Law)

The Enlightened Ones that were, and those that will be, they have Peace as their foundation.

(Sutrakrtanga: Book 1 Lecture 11: The Path)

The enlightened...monk...should preach to all the road of peace.

(The Simile of the Leaf: Uttaradhyayana)

Judaism

To the counsellors of peace is joy.

(Proverbs chapter 12 verse 20)

It is an honor for one to cease from strife.

(Proverbs chapter 20 verse 3)

Do not say, I will recompense evil; but wait on the Lord (be calm, patient and peaceful).

(Proverbs chapter 20 verse 22)

I acquaint myself with God (submit to His will) and I am at peace; by that, good shall come to me.

(Job chapter 22 verse 21)

God will keep me in perfect and constant peace as my mind is fixed on Him.

(Isaiah chapter 26 verse 3)

Sikhism

Contentment.

(One of five Sikh Virtues)

By hearing the Name (of Almighty God) truth, contentment and Divine knowledge are obtained.

(The Repetition of the Divine Name: The Japji)

Utter not one disagreeable word, since the true Lord is in

all...Distress no one's heart; every heart is a priceless jewel...If you desire God, distress no one's heart.

(Granth Sahib: Hymn by Shaikh Farid)

Taoism

Make excursion in pure simplicity...Follow the nature of things and...the world will be in peace.

(The Domain of Nothingness: Chuang Tzu)

Though troubles arise the wise are not irritated.

(Lao Tzu, Tao Te Ching (Self-Development) chapter 2)

They who have the secret of the Tao do not desire for more. Being content, they are able to mature without desire to be newly fashioned.

(Lao Tzu, Tao Te Ching (That Which Reveals *Teh* (Virtue)) chapter 15)

Seek composure (the essence of tranquillity).

(Lao Tzu, Tao Te Ching (Returning to the Source) chapter 16)

Peace and quietude are esteemed by the wise.

(Lao Tzu, Tao Te Ching (Avoiding War) chapter 31)

Those who have realized contentment are truly wealthy (in relation to spiritual treasures).

(Lao Tzu, Tao Te Ching (The Virtue (*Teh*) of Discrimination) chapter 33)

A contented person is not despised.

(Lao Tzu, Tao Te Ching (Precepts) chapter 44)

There is no misfortune greater than discontent.

(Lao Tzu, Tao Te Ching (Limitation of Desire) chapter 46)

One should resolve a difficulty while it is easy and manage a great thing while it is small. Surely all the world's difficulties arose from slight causes.

(Lao Tzu, Tao Te Ching (A Consideration of Beginnings) chapter 63)

Because they who are wise will not quarrel with anyone, no one can quarrel with them.

(Lao Tzu, Tao Te Ching (To Subordinate Self) chapter 66)

(Practicing) the virtue of not-quarrelling...is complying with Heaven. Since of old it is considered the greatest virtue (*teh*).

(Lao Tzu, Tao Te Ching (Compliance with Heaven) chapter 68)

Be content with what you have; rejoice in the way things are.

(Lao Tzu)

Zen Buddhism

To find perfect composure in the midst of change is to find Nirvana.

(Shunryu Suzuki)

Peace comes from within. Do not seek it from without.

(Zen proverb)

To be calm is the highest achievement of the self.

(Zen proverb)

To have peace in one's soul is the greatest happiness.

(*Zen proverb*)

Zoroastrianism

Contentment is the happiest condition of humanity and the most pleasing to the Creator.

(The Vision of Arda-Viraf)

Enter into no strife with those of evil repute.

(Admonitions)

Chapter 28

Purity (Holiness)

Purity is cleanliness of the mind, spirit and heart; holiness and saintliness; freedom from evil, corruption, a propensity to harm or hurt others and negativity. Purity is childlike innocence, chastity and an intense love and mindfulness of God. If we wish to respect the immanent quality of God within each of us, we must strive for internal purity and cultivate a clean and peaceful soul. Rather than being preoccupied, and even obsessed, with the superficial and transient outer physical or material image, we should focus instead on enhancing the beauty, light and splendor of the Divine inner person and eternal soul. Purification of the inner self or spirit, which only we can do gradually with Divine assistance, is attainable through the pursuit of the Divine Virtues, the abandonment of that which is spiritually harmful and the adoption of that which is wholesome. The wise soul readily and humbly accepts Divine guidance and correction along the steep pathway to holiness. Let good thoughts, good words and righteous deeds be one's mantra. Avoid the stains, blemishes and defilements of the soul through moderation and restraint of the senses.

Excessive attachment to objects, persons or ambitions through desire, passion or ignorance pollutes the mind, and when it generates negative, destructive and unethical thoughts, feelings and emotions, the mind inclines to impurity. A releasing of the mind from wrongdoing and such excessive attachment causes it to generate more positive, constructive and ethical thoughts and facilitates a deeper mindfulness towards God and a blossoming of God's Love within the heart.

Become like the clean and pure lotus, despite residing in the muddy waters of this worldly realm (Buddhist proverb).

Scriptural References

Baha'i

Your heart is My (God's) Home; purify it.

(Of Divine Humanity: Words of Wisdom from the Supreme Pen of Baha'u'llah)

All must serve God with purity and virtue...Some are content with words; but the truth of words is tested by deeds.

(Of Knowledge: Words of Wisdom from the Supreme Pen of Baha'u'llah)

Buddhism

One does not become pure by washing, as do the mortals in this world; one who casts away every sin, great and small, is a brahmin who has cast off sin.

(Udanavarga chapter 33 verse 13)

All that we are is the result of what we have thought...If one speaks or acts with a pure mind, happiness follows them as one's shadow.

(The Dhammapada chapter 1 (The Twin-Verses) verse 2)

They who have cleansed themselves from sin, are well grounded in all virtues and endowed also with temperance (restraint/moderation) and truth: they are indeed worthy of the yellow dress (monkhood).

(The Dhammapada chapter 1 (The Twin-Verses) verse 10)

Purity and impurity depend on oneself. No one can purify another.

(The Dhammapada chapter 12 (Self) verse 165)

By degrees, little by little, from moment to moment, the wise remove their own impurities, as a smith removes the dross of silver.

(The Dhammapada chapter 18 (Impurity) verse 239)

All created things perish. When one sees this in wisdom, then one becomes dispassionate towards the painful. This is the way to purity.

(The Dhammapada chapter 20 (The Way) verse 277)

Watchful of speech, well restrained in mind, let one do no wrong with the body; let one purify these three ways of action, and attain the way (to Purity) made known by the wise.

(The Dhammapada chapter 20 (The Way) verse 281)

Christianity

Blessed are the pure in heart, for they will see God.

(Matthew chapter 5 verse 8)

The kingdom of God is within you.

(Luke chapter 17 verse 21)

Let us cleanse ourselves from all filthiness of the flesh and spirit, perfecting holiness in the fear of God.

(2 Corinthians chapter 7 verse 1)

Flee...youthful lusts: but follow righteousness, faith, charity, peace, with those who call on the Lord out of a pure heart.

(2 Timothy chapter 2 verse 22)

I always...discipline myself (deadening my carnal and bodily appetites and worldly desires) to have a clear conscience, void of offence towards God and towards (humanity).

(Acts chapter 24 verse 16)

My body is the temple (sanctuary) of the Holy Spirit Who lives within me, Whom I have received (as a gift) from God.

(1 Corinthians chapter 6 verse 19)

Follow peace with all and holiness, without which no one will see the Lord.

(Hebrews chapter 12 verse 14)

I live in obedience to God; I do not conform myself to the evil desires (that governed me) in my former ignorance. The One Who called me is holy and I am also holy in all my conduct and manner of living.

(1 Peter chapter 1 verses 14-15)

Confucianism

If one has the will to get rid of evil, one should resist evil right in the things one is doing. Getting rid of evil is to rectify what is incorrect in the mind.

(The Investigation of the Mind: Wang Yang-ming's Conversations with Huang I-fang)

Gandhi

God can never be realized by one who is not pure of heart.

(Mohandas Gandhi, *An Autobiography*)

The path of self-purification is hard and steep. To attain to perfect purity one has to become absolutely passion-free in thought, speech and action.

(Mohandas Gandhi, *An Autobiography*)

Hinduism

Purity of mind.

(Saintly Virtue No. 2 of those endowed with a Divine Nature: Bhagavad-Gita chapter 16 verses 1-3)

I am...what purifies, the sacred syllable *Om* (God).

(Everything is a Sacrifice to Me: Bhagavad-Gita chapter 9)

Utter speech purified by truth, keep the heart pure.

(The Laws of Manu: Manava-dharma-sastra chapter 6 verses 33-60)

Islam

Truly, God loves those who keep themselves pure.

(The Cow chapter 2 verse 222)

You who believe, do not walk in Satan's footsteps...But for God's grace and mercy, none of you would ever have kept themselves pure. But God purifies whom He will; God hears all and knows all.

(The Light chapter 24 verse 21)

For those who follow the right path, God increases their

guidance and bestows on them their piety.

(Muhammad or The Fighting chapter 47 verse 17)

Do not pretend to purity; God knows best those who guard themselves against evil.

(The Star chapter 53 verse 32)

Prosperous are they who purify their soul.

(The Sun chapter 91 verse 9)

Those who spend their wealth in giving charity as self-purification...will surely be well pleased (when they enter Paradise).

(The Night chapter 92 verses 18-21)

Jainism

The pious (holy) obtain purity and the pure stand firmly in the Law (Teaching): the soul afterwards reaches the highest Nirvana (ascending heavens).

(Uttaradhyayana: Third Lecture: The Four Requisites)

Those who are impure and vain...are wholly under the influence (of their passions). Despising them as unholy (persons), desire virtues till the end of your life.

(Uttaradhyayana: Fourth Lecture: Impurity)

The pious show an island to the beings which are carried away by the flood of (earthly) existence and suffer for their deeds.

(Sutrakrtanga: Book 1 Eleventh Lecture: The Path)

Judaism

I consecrate myself therefore and I will be holy; for He is the Lord my God.

(Leviticus chapter 20 verse 7)

Every word of God is pure.

(Proverbs chapter 30 verse 5)

Sikhism

Live cleanly.

(Nanak's Call: A Janamsakhi)

The Lord entered my being, I made pilgrimage within myself and was purified.

(Spiritual Marriage: The Bara Mah)

They who hear and obey and love God in their heart, shall wash off their impurity.

(Guru Nanak's Japji)

When the mind is defiled by sin, it is cleansed by the love of the (sacred Divine) Name.

(Guru Nanak's Japji)

Taoism

By purifying the subconscious desires, one may be without fault.

(Lao Tzu, Tao Te Ching (What is Possible) chapter 10)

Let all...hold to that which is reliable, namely cherish purity.

(Lao Tzu, Tao Te Ching (Return to Simplicity) chapter 19)

The Ten (Native American) Indian Commandments

Look after the well-being of mind and body.

(Commandment No. 7)

Zoroastrianism

Learn purity.

(Admonitions)

Purity is the best good.

(Khordah-Avesta)

Make thyself pure, O righteous man! Anyone in the world here below can win purity for himself, namely, when he cleanses himself with good thoughts, good words and good deeds.

(Prayer of Ashem Vohu)

Chapter 29

Quietude

Quietude is quietness/stillness of the mind and economy and simplicity in speech and in the manner in which one conducts their life. The quality of being taciturn, that is, inclined to silence or reserved in speech, facilitates engagement in deeper contemplative/meditative prayer. There is a noble dignity and profound peace in silence. The incessantly talkative are slow to learn and acquire wisdom, but those who are silent speak (even teach), have wisdom, knowledge, observational insight and understanding. They who shut their lips understand (Proverbs chapter 17 verse 28). Silence indeed can speak volumes. And the quieter one becomes, the more one will be able to hear (Zen proverb) and to listen more attentively and empathetically to the stories of others. In the innermost depths of silence will be revealed our connection to everything that has ever been and everything that ever will be.

It is therefore no accident that people tend to listen more closely to those who speak less, as their words carry more authority and energy. A soft tongue breaks the bone (Proverbs chapter 25 verse 15). Do not speak, then, unless it improves on silence (Buddhist proverb).

Scriptural References

Buddhism
Those who meditate with diligence attain much happiness.
(The Dhammapada chapter 2 (On Earnestness) verse 27)

Christianity
Lead a quiet and peaceable life in all godliness and honesty.

(1 Timothy chapter 2 verse 2)
A meek and quiet spirit is in the sight of God of great praise.
(1 Peter chapter 3 verse 4)

Confucianism
Silence is a true friend who never betrays.
(Confucius)

Desiderata
Go placidly amid the noise and haste and remember what peace there may be in silence.
(Verse 1)

Islam
God's messenger (the Prophet Muhammad) was far from talkative.
(Abu Muhammad al-Husayn, Mishkat al-Masabih)

Jainism
One should...not be talkative in the presence of the wise.
(Uttaradhyayana: First Lecture: On Discipline)
In speaking (a monk) should use as few words as possible.
(Sutrakrtanga: Book 1 Lecture 9: The Law)

Judaism
Do not be rash with your mouth and do not let your heart be hasty to utter any thing before God: for God is in Heaven and you are upon the earth: therefore let your words be few.
(Ecclesiastes chapter 5 verse 2)
To control one's mouth is wise.
(Proverbs chapter 10 verse 19)
They who control their mouth keep their life: but they who open wide their lips shall have destruction.
(Proverbs chapter 13 verse 3)

Better is a dry morsel and quietness therewith, than a house full of strife.

(Proverbs chapter 17 verse 1)

One who has knowledge uses words sparingly.

(Proverbs chapter 17 verse 27)

They who shut their lips are esteemed persons of understanding.

(Proverbs chapter 17 verse 28)

A soft tongue breaks the bone.

(Proverbs chapter 25 verse 15)

In quietness and trust is my strength.

(Isaiah chapter 30 verse 15)

Taoism

They who have reached the stage of thought (enlightenment) are silent. They who have attained to perfect knowledge are also silent. They who use silence in lieu of speech really do speak.

(Blankness of Mind: Lieh Tzu)

The wise are not conspicuous in their affairs or given to much talking.

(Lao Tzu, Tao Te Ching (Self-Development) chapter 2)

To win true merit...the personality must be retiring (reserved/shy). This is the heavenly Tao.

(Lao Tzu, Tao Te Ching (Moderation) chapter 9)

We can clarify troubled waters by slowly quieting them.

(Lao Tzu, Tao Te Ching (That Which Reveals *Teh* (Virtue)) chapter 15)

Taciturnity is natural to (humanity). A whirlwind never outlasts the morning, nor a violent rain the day.

(Lao Tzu, Tao Te Ching (Emptiness and Not-Doing (*Wu Wei*)) chapter 23)

If desire be absent there is quietness.

(Lao Tzu, Tao Te Ching (Administering the Government) chapter 37)

Those who close their mouth...will be free from trouble to the end of life.

(Lao Tzu, Tao Te Ching (Return to Origin) chapter 52)

The one who knows does not speak; the one who speaks does not know.

(Lao Tzu, Tao Te Ching (The *Teh* (Virtue) of the Mysterious) chapter 56)

Silence is a source of great strength.

(Lao Tzu)

Zen Buddhism

Sometimes it takes...noise to appreciate silence.

(Zen proverb)

The quieter you become, the more you are able to hear (listen).

(Zen proverb)

Sit quietly doing nothing. Spring comes and the grass grows by itself.

(Zen proverb)

We sat together, the forest and I, merging into silence. Until only the forest remained.

(Li Po)

Chapter 30

Repentance and Atonement

Reflection upon, and acknowledgment of, one's errors and past mistakes and wrongdoing provide opportunities for spiritual growth.

Repentance is the feeling of genuine and heartfelt contrition for past misconduct and its harmful consequences (suffered by the perpetrator and victims); atonement is providing reparation or making amends for the injury caused by such misconduct. Through a process of internal self-review of one's life (which does not seek to judge or condemn but rather to awaken), the causes of wrongdoing may be identified, understood and renounced and personal responsibility accepted for one's actions and omissions.

Repentance from the tongue must be accompanied by a repentance from the heart. Repentance without renunciation is of no avail. Genuinely and sincerely confessing and repenting one's sins in mind, speech and body and seeking God's forgiveness and guidance on how to avoid future wrong, heal and restore the right relationship between the believer and God and constitute a form of spiritual renewal or fresh start going forward. Through acceptance of responsibility and penance (for example, fasting, abstinence or doing righteousness) comes absolution.

Scriptural References

Baha'i

You must pray and repent for all that you have done which is wrong; and you must implore and ask for help and assistance; so that you may continue to make (spiritual) progress.

(True Belief: Words of Wisdom from the Supreme Pen of Baha'u'llah)

Buddhism

Evil-doers mourn in this world and they mourn in the next; they mourn in both. They mourn and suffer when they see the evil result of their own work.

(The Dhammapada chapter 1 (The Twin-Verses) verse 15)

If...any monk shall remember a sin and not reveal it, it will be a conscious falsehood. But a conscious falsehood...has been declared by the Blessed One to be a deadly sin. Therefore, if a monk remembers having committed a sin and desires again to be pure, let them reveal the sin committed and when it has been revealed, it shall be well for them.

(Vinaya, Mahavagga, Second Khandhaka, chapter II.3.3)

Christianity

There is joy in the presence of the angels of God over one sinner who repents.

(Luke chapter 15 verse 10)

If we confess our sins, God is faithful and just to forgive us our sins and to cleanse us from all unrighteousness. If we say that we have not sinned, we make Him a liar and His word is not in us.

(1 John chapter 1 verses 9-10)

Islam

Truly, God loves those who turn to Him in repentance.

(The Cow chapter 2 verse 222)

God will not call you to account for that which is unintentional...but He will call you to account for what you mean in your hearts.

(The Cow chapter 2 verse 225)

Our Lord! Forgive us our sins and expiate from us our evil

deeds and let us die with the righteous.

(The Family of Imran chapter 3 verse 193)

Of no effect is the repentance of those who continue to do evil deeds.

(The Women chapter 4 verse 18)

Whosoever repents after their crime and makes amends by doing righteous good deeds, then verily God will accept their repentance. Know that God is forgiving and merciful.

(The Table chapter 5 verse 39)

Those who committed evil deeds and then repented afterwards and believed, verily, your Lord is forgiving and merciful.

(The Heights (or The Wall with Elevations) chapter 7 verse 153)

God accepts repentance from His servants and takes (atonement alms)...God Alone is the One Who forgives and is merciful.

(The Repentance chapter 9 verse 104)

Seek the forgiveness of your Lord and turn to Him in repentance, that He may...bestow on you His abounding Grace.

((Prophet) Hud chapter 11 verse 3)

God guides to Himself those who turn to Him in repentance.

(The Thunder chapter 13 verse 27)

God is forgiving to those who turn to Him in repentance.

(The Journey by Night chapter 17 verse 25)

Those who repent and believe and do righteous work – those, God will change their evil deeds into good deeds, for God is ever forgiving and merciful; and whosoever repents and does righteousness, they truly turn to God in repentance.

(The Discrimination chapter 25 verses 70-1)

God accepts the repentance of His servants and pardons their sins. He has knowledge of all your actions.

(The Counsel chapter 42 verse 25)

Jainism

As life is so fleet and existence so precarious, wipe off

(acknowledge and renounce or confess) the sins you ever committed.

(The Simile of the Leaf: Uttaradhyayana)

Leave off (renounce or repudiate) the causes of sin.

(The Simile of the Leaf: Uttaradhyayana)

I must confess my day-to-day transgressions of the mind, speech and body, through anger, pride, deceit or greed, false behaviour and neglect of the Teaching and whatever offence I have committed I here confess, repudiate and repent of it and set aside my past deeds.

(Reverence for the Order: Vandana Formula)

For the sake of the splendour, honor and glory of this life, for the sake of birth, death and final liberation, for the removal of pain, all causes of sin are to be comprehended and renounced in this world. They who, in this world, comprehend and renounce these causes of sin are called a sage.

(Acaranga Sutra: First Book Lecture 1: Knowledge of the Weapon)

In this world the causes of sin must be comprehended and renounced. Those who do not comprehend and renounce the causes of sin are born again and again in manifold births and experience all painful feelings.

(Acaranga Sutra: First Book Lecture 1: Knowledge of the Weapon)

As long as I live, I confess and repent my sins...in mind, speech and body.

(First Great Vow: Acaranga Sutra)

Judaism

In repentance and rest is my salvation, in quietness and trust is my strength.

(Isaiah chapter 30 verse 15)

I will declare my iniquity; I will be sorry (remorseful) for my sin.

(Psalms chapter 38 verse 18)

Those who (cover up) their sins shall not prosper: but whoso confesses and forsakes them shall have mercy (forgiveness).

(Proverbs chapter 28 verse 13)

Sikhism

Pardon our errors and mistakes.

(Sri Wahguru Ji Ki Fatah!)

Taoism

The Tao is the good person's (spiritual) treasure, the bad person's last resort...The reason the Ancients esteemed Tao was because if sought (asked for like wisdom) it was obtained and because by it those who have sin could be saved.

(Lao Tzu, Tao Te Ching (The Practice of Tao) chapter 62)

The Ten (Native American) Indian Commandments

Take full responsibility for your actions.

(Commandment No. 10)

Zen Buddhism

Failing is not always failure. Mistakes are opportunities for growth.

(Zen proverb)

Zoroastrianism

The Law of Ahura-Mazda (God), O Zarathustra (Zoroaster)! takes away from those who confess it the bonds of their sin.

(Forgiveness of Sin)

The Law of Ahura-Mazda cleanses the faithful from every evil thought, word and deed, as a swift-rushing, mighty wind cleanses the plain. So let all deeds you do be henceforth good...A full atonement for your sin is effected by means of the Law of Ahura-Mazda.

(The Law of Ahura-Mazda)

But when the person who is damned dies, for three days and nights does their soul hover near their head and weeps, saying, "Where shall I go and in whom shall I now take refuge?" And during these three days and nights they see with their eyes all the sins and wickedness that they committed on earth.

(The Cinvat Bridge: Menok i Khrat)

All that I ought to have thought and have not thought, all that I ought to have said and have not said, all that I ought to have done and have not done...all that I ought not to have thought and yet have thought, all that I ought not to have spoken and yet have spoken, all that I ought not to have done and yet have done...for thoughts, words and works (deeds), bodily and spiritual, earthly and heavenly, pray I for forgiveness and repent of it.

(Prayer for Repentance)

Chapter 31

Restraint (Self-Control/Moderation) of the Senses

Restraint is keeping in check or under control our desires and passions. It involves moderation, temperance and an avoidance of extremes – excess and insufficiency – through balance (akin to the Buddhist concept of The Middle Way or Middle Path). In this context, we are referring to self-mastery of the mind and of the senses, through the avoidance of overindulgence of desires and passions and the temptation to retaliate. Our senses lure us to seek instant pleasure and gratification but treading the narrow pathway to God requires us to forgo cravings and sensual and material pleasures in order to walk a life in the spirit. To paraphrase Jesus of Nazareth, what is of the flesh is flesh and what is of the Spirit is spirit (New Testament: John chapter 3 verse 6). Restraint of the senses and passions and forsaking sensual pleasures draws one closer to the spiritual realm and the gateway to God and Truth.

Several Eastern faiths aptly and succinctly express this Divine Virtue through the concept of control of the mind (thinking processes), speech and conduct (actions). This respectively requires us to be actuated by pure or clean motives and good thoughts and intentions so that we do not cause harm or offence to others and do not prejudge them (that is, to be liberated from our own preconceptions and prejudices); to adopt edifying and uplifting language and avoid lying, slander, gossip, boasting, rude and negative comments and incitement of evil; and to avoid killing, stealing, promiscuity and other offences towards God. From good thoughts (the upstream) flow good words and deeds (the downstream). When we harbor negative thoughts of others, we harm our soul as we are all God's creatures, our souls possessing a spark of the Divine Love.

Thoughts and words create our reality and experiences. What we create inside us is lived out externally. Self-mastery is therefore one of the greatest personal achievements one could ever aspire to.

Scriptural References

Baha'i
Moderation is desirable in every affair.

(Tablet of Baha'u'llah: Words of Paradise)

Extinguish (My Light within you) not with the contrary winds of desires and passions.

(Of the Light: Words of Wisdom from the Supreme Pen of Baha'u'llah)

Do not let the desires of the self (ego) find a place within you; for it is certain that even when you reach the highest state of spirituality, one worldly desire can cause your downfall. The spirit is like a bird; when it flies in the air it is always (ascending), but the self is like a hunter, who is thinking how to catch the bird. You will see that by one arrow, one shot, it will be brought low. This arrow is the connection with this world...the desires of this world; the honors of this world. In many ways the hunter will stop the spirit from ascending. That is why you must ask and implore and entreat, "O God, protect me from myself!"

(True Belief: Words of Wisdom from the Supreme Pen of Baha'u'llah)

Buddhism
Do not be devoted to the pleasures of sense which is the way of the world.

(The First Sermon: Vinaya, Mahavagga)

Avoid sexual misconduct.

(Third Basic Precept)

Of these two gifts (the carnal/flesh and the spiritual), the spiritual is pre-eminent.

(Itivuttaka chapter 4 verse 1)

All that we are is the result of what we have thought: it is founded on our thoughts, it is made up of our thoughts. If one speaks or acts with an evil thought, pain follows them, as the wheel follows the foot of the ox that draws the carriage.

(The Dhammapada chapter 1 (The Twin-Verses) verse 1)

As no rain leaks into a well-roofed house, passion does not invade a cultivated mind.

(The Dhammapada chapter 1 (The Twin-Verses) verse 14)

Have no intimacy with sense pleasures. Those who meditate with diligence attain much happiness.

(The Dhammapada chapter 2 (On Earnestness) verse 27)

A controlled mind brings happiness.

(The Dhammapada chapter 3 (Thought) verse 35)

Those who gather only the flowers (of sense pleasures) and whose mind is distracted, death carries them away as a flood carries off a sleeping village.

(The Dhammapada chapter 4 (Flowers) verse 47)

They whose senses are mastered like horses well under the charioteer's control, they are free from pride, free from appetites, such a one even the gods envy.

(The Dhammapada chapter 7 (The Venerable/Arhat) verse 94)

Better is it truly to conquer oneself than to conquer others. Nothing can turn into defeat the victory of a person such as this who is self-mastered and ever restrained in conduct.

(The Dhammapada chapter 8 (The Thousands) verses 104-5)

To speak no ill, to do no harm, to practise restraint according to the fundamental precepts, to be moderate in eating, to dwell on the highest thoughts, this is the Teaching of the Awakened.

(The Dhammapada chapter 14 (The Buddha/The Awakened) verse 185)

From lust arises grief; from lust arises fear. For those who are free from lust there is no grief, no fear.

(The Dhammapada chapter 16 (Pleasure) verse 215)

Watchful of speech, well restrained in mind, do no evil with the body.

(The Dhammapada chapter 20 (The Way) verse 281)

Good is restraint of the eye. Good is restraint of the ear. Good is restraint of the nose. Good is restraint of the tongue. Good is restraint of the body. Good is restraint in speech. Good is restraint in thought. Restraint in all things is good.

(The Dhammapada chapter 25 (The Bhikshu/Mendicant) verses 360-1)

If anyone should give you a blow with their hand, you should abandon any (retaliatory) desires and utter no evil words.

(Majjhima Nikaya chapter 21 verse 6)

Not falling into wrong views, virtuous and endowed with insight, one gives up attachment to sense-desires. Verily one does not return to enter a womb again (is not reincarnated).

(Sutta Nipata: 1 Uragavagga 8 Mettasutta 10 verse 151)

Nothing can harm you as much as your own thoughts unguarded.

(The Buddha)

I am unable to restrain external phenomena, but I shall restrain my own mind.

(Shantideva)

Christianity

That which is born of the flesh is flesh; and that which is born of the (Holy) Spirit is spirit.

(John chapter 3 verse 6)

If anyone strikes you on the cheek, offer the other also.

(Luke chapter 6 verse 29)

The good person out of the good treasure of the heart produces good and the evil person out of the evil treasure of their heart produces evil; for it is out of the abundance of the heart that the mouth speaks.

(Luke chapter 6 verse 45)

Take heed to yourselves (be cautious), lest at any time your hearts be overcharged with surfeiting (excess in eating) and drunkenness and cares of this life (worries, anxieties and distractions).

(Luke chapter 21 verse 34)

It is not what goes into the mouth that defiles a person; but that which comes out of the mouth, this defiles a person.

(Matthew chapter 15 verse 11)

Those things which proceed out of the mouth come forth from the heart; and they defile a person. For out of the heart proceed evil thoughts, murders, adulteries, fornications, blasphemies. These are the things which defile a person: but to eat with unwashed hands does not defile a person.

(Matthew chapter 15 verses 18-20)

Walk in the (Holy) Spirit; do not succumb to impulses of a carnal nature.

(Romans chapter 8 verse 8)

Let no corrupt communication proceed out of your mouth, but that which is good to the use of edifying (building up or increasing the faith), that it may deliver grace to the hearers.

(Ephesians chapter 4 verse 29)

Be not drunk with wine, wherein is excess; but be filled with the (Holy) Spirit.

(Ephesians chapter 5 verse 18)

Every person who strives for...(self-) mastery is temperate (exercises moderation) in all things.

(1 Corinthians chapter 9 verse 25)

The fruit of the (Holy) Spirit is...temperance (self-control/continence).

(Galatians chapter 5 verses 22-3)

Add to your faith...temperance.

(2 Peter chapter 1 verses 5-6)

Confucianism

Have no wrong (unethical and anti-social) thoughts.

(Analects)

To cultivate the personal (spiritual) life means for the eyes not to see what is contrary to propriety, the ears not to hear what is contrary to propriety, the mouth not to say what is contrary to propriety and the four limbs not to do what is contrary to propriety.

(The Investigation of the Mind: Wang Yang-ming's Conversations with Huang I-fang)

Gandhi

To conquer the subtle passions (To achieve self-mastery) seems to me to be harder far than the physical conquest of the world by force of arms.

(Mohandas Gandhi, *An Autobiography*)

Hinduism

Control of the senses (expressed by the Hindu term *damyata* meaning restraint or self-control).

(Saintly Virtue No. 5 of those endowed with a Divine Nature: Bhagavad-Gita chapter 16 verses 1-3)

Wisdom is swept away by manifold desires.

(Bhagavad-Gita chapter 7)

Whatever you do in self-restraint, do as an offering to me. Thus you will be freed from the prison of deeds and their results... Wholly trained in renunciation (release from attachments and desires)...you will come to (God).

(Everything is a Sacrifice to Me: Bhagavad-Gita chapter 9)

According as one acts, so does one become.

(Brhadaranyaka Upanisad)

Let one not, out of desire (for enjoyments), attach oneself to sensual pleasures and let one carefully obviate an excessive attachment to them.

(The Laws of Manu: Manava-dharma-sastra chapter 4 verses 1-18)

One should practise...self-restraint (*damyata*).

(The Three Da's: Brhadaranyaka Upanisad)

Islam

It is better for you to practise self-restraint.

(The Women chapter 4 verse 25)

God loves not the extravagant.

(The Cattle chapter 6 verse 141)

Do not squander your wealth wastefully.

(The Journey by Night chapter 17 verse 26)

Be neither miserly nor prodigal (wastefully or recklessly extravagant), for then you should either earn reproach or be reduced to penury.

(The Journey by Night chapter 17 verse 29)

Avoid fornication; surely it is an abomination and evil as a way.

(The Journey by Night chapter 17 verse 32)

Do not be too loud in your prayer or too quiet, but seek a middle way.

(The Journey by Night chapter 17 verse 110)

Have you (O Prophet Muhammad) seen those who have taken as their god their own vain desire?

(The Discrimination chapter 25 verse 43)

The servants of the Merciful God are those who, when they expend, are neither recklessly extravagant nor miserly, but always hold a medium between those (extremes).

(The Discrimination chapter 25 verse 67)

God's Messenger (the Prophet Muhammad) said: "Always adopt a middle, moderate, regular course whereby you will reach (Paradise)."

(Sahih Al-Bukhari 8/6463 (O.P. 470))

God's Messenger (the Prophet Muhammad) said: "Whoever

can guarantee (the chastity of) what is between the two jaw-bones and what is between the two legs, I guarantee Paradise for them."
(Sahih Al-Bukhari 8/6474 (O.P. 481))

Jainism
Though one may believe in the Law (Teaching), one will rarely practise it; for people are engrossed by pleasures.
(The Simile of the Leaf: Uttaradhyayana)
An ascetic should (practise restraint) and shake off sinfulness.
(The Simile of the Leaf: Uttaradhyayana)
Having heard the Law humans will combat their passions.
(The Simile of the Leaf: Uttaradhyayana)
The enlightened monk should be controlled.
(The Simile of the Leaf: Uttaradhyayana)
One should practise self-control.
(Uttaradhyayana: Thirty-First Lecture: Mode of Life)
A monk should only answer after ripe (due) reflection.
(Sutrakrtanga: Book 1 Lecture 9: The Law)
The wise restrain their senses. They should do no harm to anybody, neither by thoughts, nor words, nor acts.
(Sutrakrtanga: Book 1 Eleventh Lecture: The Path)
A sage always restrained and subduing their senses brings about Beatitude (supreme blessedness), free of defiling influences. Those who do not know this Law are not awakened (enlightened).
(Sutrakrtanga: Book 1 Eleventh Lecture: The Path)
I renounce all sensual pleasures...I shall not give way to sensuality.
(Fourth Great Vow: Acaranga Sutra)

Judaism
I am not rash with my mouth.
(Ecclesiastes chapter 5 verse 2)
A fool throws off restraint and is careless.

(Proverbs chapter 14 verse 16)

Those who have a perverse tongue fall into mischief.

(Proverbs chapter 17 verse 20)

A fool's mouth leads to destruction.

(Proverbs chapter 18 verse 7)

Those who restrain their mouth and tongue protect their soul from troubles.

(Proverbs chapter 21 verse 23)

Have you found honey? Eat only so much as is sufficient (necessary) for you, lest you be filled therewith and vomit it.

(Proverbs chapter 25 verse 16)

Those who have no rule (self-control/discipline) over their own spirit are like a city that is broken down and without walls (vulnerable).

(Proverbs chapter 25 verse 28)

Do not respond to fools according to their folly, lest you also become like them.

(Proverbs chapter 26 verse 4)

Shintoism

Bear yourselves in modesty and moderation.

(The Japanese Ethos: Imperial Rescript on Education 30 October 1890 (modernized Shinto))

Sikhism

Lust.

(One of five Sikh deadly sins)

O God, save us from the sin of lust.

(The Community and its Past Saints: A Congregational Prayer)

From the evils of worldly and sensual love and from the sin of desire preserve us.

(Prayer by Guru Arjan)

Taoism

The mouths (of those who seek immortality) must never encourage evil.

(The Reward for Deeds: p'ao-p'u Tzu)

Not to desire the things of sense (of the five senses) is to know the freedom of spirituality; and to desire is to learn the limitations of matter (the flesh).

(Lao Tzu, Tao Te Ching (What is the Tao) chapter 1)

Ignoring the things which awaken desire keeps the heart at rest.

(Lao Tzu, Tao Te Ching (Quieting People) chapter 3)

Continuing to fill a pail after it is full, the water will be wasted.

(Lao Tzu, Tao Te Ching (Moderation) chapter 9)

By self-control one can unify (develop or build up) the character.

(Lao Tzu, Tao Te Ching (What is Possible) chapter 10)

An excess of light blinds the eye; an excess of noise ruins the ear; an excess of condiments deadens the taste.

(Lao Tzu, Tao Te Ching (Avoiding Desire) chapter 12)

Let all...hold to that which is reliable, namely...diminish one's desire.

(Lao Tzu, Tao Te Ching (Return to Simplicity) chapter 19)

Those who seek to grasp it, will lose it. Therefore the wise (person) practices moderation, abandoning pleasure, extravagance and indulgence.

(Lao Tzu, Tao Te Ching (Not Forcing Things (*Wu Wei*)) chapter 29)

They who are able to conquer others have force, but they who are able to control themselves are mighty.

(Lao Tzu, Tao Te Ching (The Virtue (*Teh*) of Discrimination) chapter 33)

Extreme indulgence certainly greatly wastes. Much hoarding certainly invites severe loss.

(Lao Tzu, Tao Te Ching (Precepts) chapter 44)

There is no sin greater than desire.

(Lao Tzu, Tao Te Ching (Limitation of Desire) chapter 46)

They who shut their sense gates (restrain their senses) will be free from trouble to the end of life.

(Lao Tzu, Tao Te Ching (Return to Origin) chapter 52)

To be excessive in eating and drinking is to know the pride of robbers. This is contrary to Tao (the Way).

(Lao Tzu, Tao Te Ching (Gain by Insight) chapter 53)

In worshipping Heaven, nothing surpasses moderation... (possessing moderation) is like having deep roots and a strong stem.

(Lao Tzu, Tao Te Ching (To Keep Tao) chapter 59)

The wise desire to be free from desire.

(Lao Tzu, Tao Te Ching (Consider the Insignificant) chapter 64)

Zoroastrianism

No pleasure but has its concomitant pain. Roses have thorns and honours fall into disgrace. It is pleasant to drink wine, but intoxication brings pain, if not disgrace; if you exceed in eating, this also brings its punishment...therefore let the avoidance of excess in everything be most particularly inculcated...(over-indulgences) encourage the most deadly sins and the soul so indulging will most assuredly be cut off from Heaven...the indulgence of our passions brings no pleasure of long duration, or impresses any good sentiment on the heart.

(The Vision of Arda-Viraf)

The world is composed of lust, avarice and of passions the most ungovernable; if God gives them one thing, even that for which they most desire, they are not satisfied, but are continually craving for more and more.

(The Vision of Arda-Viraf)

Commit no lustfulness, so that harm and regret may not reach you from your own actions.

(Commandments for the Body and the Soul)

Regarding wine (intoxicants), it is evident that it is possible for good and bad temper to manifest through wine...one must be cautious as to the moderate drinking thereof.

(Temperance)

I praise the well-thought, well-spoken, well-performed thoughts, words and works [deeds]...I abandon all evil thoughts, words and works.

(The Creed)

(Referring to the Divine judgment of the soul after death) I (a representation of a beautiful young woman) am your good thoughts, good words and good deeds which you did think and say and do (during the departed's lifetime).

(The Cinvat Bridge: Menok i Khrat)

Chapter 32

Righteousness

Righteousness is not self-righteousness. Righteousness is the Divine quality of being virtuous, just, sincere, penitent, pious and morally upright; of possessing true goodness, truthfulness, mercy, charitableness and integrity. Righteousness is heeding the deep inner voice of one's conscience and doing what one instinctively knows to be right, ethical and moral.

Righteousness perceives value in everyone and everything and treats everyone and everything with goodness. It is an attribute of those who are in right standing and relationship with God. Acts of righteousness must be spiritually authentic, well-motivated and altruistic (as opposed to being done ostentatiously or actuated by an ulterior motive such as gaining earthly praise or fame).

One should act rather from their highest self and their noblest of instincts, seeking an outcome that will attain the highest good for all concerned. What you give, you receive; so render goodness and it will be returned to you. It will give you satisfaction in this life and follow your soul into eternity.

Scriptural References

Baha'i
If you see one who is truthful, who really believes and is just, who is attracted to the Kingdom (of Heaven) and whose will (self) is annihilated (surrendered) in the Way of God; then you will know that they are a tree of the Kingdom.

(True Belief: Words of Wisdom from the Supreme Pen of Baha'u'llah)

Buddhism

Let the wise...do righteousness...a treasure (of the heart) which does not pass away.

(Khuddakapatha chapter 8 verse 9)

Even the righteous experience evil days until their good deeds ripen (mature). But when they bear fruit, then they see the happy results.

(The Dhammapada chapter 9 (Evil) verse 120)

Do not think lightly of good, saying: "It will not come near to me." Even as a water-pot is filled by the falling of drops, so the wise, gathering it drop by drop, fill (themselves) with good.

(The Dhammapada chapter 9 (Evil) verse 122)

Overcome evil by good.

(The Dhammapada chapter 17 (Anger) verse 223)

Christianity

Blessed are they who hunger and thirst after righteousness: for they shall be filled.

(Matthew chapter 5 verse 6)

Everyone who does evil hates the light, neither comes to the light, but their deeds shall be reproved. But they who do truth (obey God's Law/Commandments) come to the light, that their deeds may be made manifest, that they are wrought (fashioned or formed) in God.

(John chapter 3 verse 20-1)

Follow after righteousness.

(1 Timothy chapter 6 verse 11)

Confucianism

Uprightness and Goodness.

(Two of the five Confucian Virtues)

Righteousness (i) is the principle of setting things right and proper.

(The Well-Ordered Society: Doctrine of the Mean)

The feeling of shame (experienced through the exercise of the Divine Virtue of Conscience) is the beginning of righteousness.

(The Innateness of the Four Great Virtues: Mencius)

When good is done, evil is corrected…In this way the innate knowledge of our mind will not be obscured by selfish desires and can then be extended to the utmost.

(The Investigation of the Mind: Wang Yang-ming's Conversations with Huang I-fang)

Hinduism

Virtue (spiritual treasures of the heart) alone will follow (the soul after death), wherever (the soul) may go, therefore do your duty (of obeying the Sacred Scriptures) unflinchingly.

(Vaisnava-dharma-sastra chapter 20 verses 39-53)

Islam

Whatsoever you do of good deeds, truly, God knows it well.

(The Cow chapter 2 verse 215)

(The righteous) are those who are patient, those who are truthful and devout and ask for God's forgiveness.

(The Family of Imran chapter 3 verse 17)

You cannot attain to righteousness until you give in alms of that which you cherish; and whatever of good you expend, God knows it well.

(The Family of Imran chapter 3 verse 92)

Those who give alms in prosperity and adversity, who repress their anger and who pardon others; verily, God loves those who do good.

(The Family of Imran chapter 3 verse 134)

Do good to parents, relatives, orphans, the needy and neighbours near and distant.

(The Women chapter 4 verse 36)

God loves those who do good deeds.

(The Table chapter 5 verse 93)

For those who are pious and live righteously, on them shall be no fear nor shall they grieve.

(The Heights (or The Wall with Elevations) chapter 7 verse 35)

For those who do good in this world, there is good, but their home in the Hereafter is best.

(The Bee) chapter 16 verse 30)

Your Lord knows best what is in your souls if you are righteous.

(The Journey by Night chapter 17 verse 25)

God's righteous servants will inherit the earth.

(The Prophets chapter 21 verse 105)

Those whose good deeds weigh heavy in the scales shall prosper, but those whose deeds are light shall forfeit their souls.

(The Believers chapter 23 verses 102-3)

Repel evil with good. Give to others out of what God has given to you.

(The Story chapter 28 verse 54)

And to God belongs all that is in the heavens and all that is in the earth, that He may...reward those who do good, with what is best.

(The Star chapter 53 verse 31)

Verily, those who believe in God and do righteous good deeds, for them will be gardens beneath which rivers flow (Paradise).

(The Zodiacal Signs chapter 85 verse 11)

Have We (God) not given each human being two eyes, a tongue and two lips and shown them the two paths (of right and wrong)?

(The Land chapter 90 verses 8-10)

For those who give in charity and fear God (guard themselves against evil) and believe in goodness, We (God) will smooth the path of salvation.

(The Night chapter 92 verses 5-7)

Woe to those (hypocrites) who pretend and forbid common

kindnesses.

(The Small Kindnesses chapter 107 verses 4-6)

Jainism

Righteousness consists in...giving up all kinds of passions including attachment. It is the only means of transcending the mundane existence.

(Vardhamana Mahavira)

Be eager for (self-)discipline, that you may acquire righteousness.

(Uttaradhyayana: First Lecture: On Discipline)

Judaism

My righteousness shall go before me and the glory of the Lord shall be my rear guard.

(Isaiah chapter 58 verse 8)

The righteous care for the life of their beast.

(Proverbs chapter 12 verse 10)

They who speak truth (demonstrate) righteousness.

(Proverbs chapter 12 verse 17)

The righteous hate lying.

(Proverbs chapter 13 verse 5)

The righteous find refuge through their integrity.

(Proverbs chapter 14 verse 32)

Righteousness exalts a nation: but sin is a reproach to any people.

(Proverbs chapter 14 verse 34)

The Lord...loves those who follow after righteousness.

(Proverbs chapter 15 verse 9)

Better is a little with righteousness than great revenues without right (wealth illegally or immorally accumulated).

(Proverbs chapter 16 verse 8)

The highway of the upright is to depart from evil: those who keep their way (remain on the straight and narrow path) preserve their soul.

(Proverbs chapter 16 verse 17)

The just (righteousness) walk in their integrity.

(Proverbs chapter 20 verse 7)

The righteous give and do not spare.

(Proverbs chapter 21 verse 26)

They who follow after righteousness and mercy find life, righteousness and honor.

(Proverbs chapter 21 verse 21)

Whoso walks uprightly shall be saved: but they who are perverse (evil) in their ways shall fall.

(Proverbs chapter 28 verse 18)

The righteous consider the cause (needs) of the poor: but the wicked regard not to know it.

(Proverbs chapter 29 verse 7)

Sikhism

Morality.

(One of five Sikh Virtues)

Righteousness is the offspring of mercy, which supported by patience maintains the order of nature.

(The Repetition of the Divine Name: The Japji)

How shall one become true (righteous) before God? How shall the veil of falsehood be rent? By walking, O Nanak, according to His will.

(God as Truth: Guru Nanak's Japji)

Taoism

Goodness, if it is not sincere, is not goodness.

(Lao Tzu, Tao Te Ching (Self-Development) chapter 2)

True goodness is like water, in that it benefits everything and harms nothing. Like water it always seeks the lowest place, the place that all others avoid...In generosity it is kind; in speech it is sincere...Inasmuch as it is always peaceable it is never rebuked.

(Lao Tzu, Tao Te Ching (The Nature of Goodness) chapter 8)

The wise, trusting in goodness, always save others; for them there is no outcast. Trusting in goodness, the wise save all things, for there is nothing valueless to them.

(Lao Tzu, Tao Te Ching (The Function of Skill) chapter 27)

Excessive righteousness is acting (pretending) and does thereby become pretentious.

(Lao Tzu, Tao Te Ching (A Discussion About *Teh* (Virtue)) chapter 38)

The good (the wise person) treats with goodness; the not-good the wise also treats with goodness, for *teh* (virtue) is goodness.

(Lao Tzu, Tao Te Ching (The Virtue (*Teh*) of Trust) chapter 49)

They who have virtue (*teh*) keep their obligations; they who have no virtue insist on their rights. Tao of Heaven has no favorites but always helps the good person.

(Lao Tzu, Tao Te Ching (Enforcing Contracts) chapter 79)

The Ten (Native American) Indian Commandments
Do what you know to be right.

(Commandment No. 6)

Wavoka's Letter
Do right always. It will give you satisfaction in life.

(The Ghost Dance)

Zen Buddhism
Life is an echo. What you send out, comes back. What you sow, you reap. What you give, you get. What you see in others, exists in you. Remember, life is an echo. It always gets back to you. So give goodness.

(Zen proverb)

Zoroastrianism

Those who perform good works will have their reward in eternal life.

(The Vision of Arda-Viraf)

In performing good works you should be diligent, so that it may come to your assistance among the spirits (in the Hereafter).

(Commandments for the Body and the Soul)

Combat adversaries with right (righteousness).

(Admonitions)

Chapter 33

Simplicity

Apart from an absence of luxury or pretentiousness, simplicity denotes innocence, naturalness, openness, humility, sincerity or genuineness and artlessness (an absence of deceit, cunning and craftiness); a lack of shrewdness and worldly cleverness; unassuming straightforwardness. Simplicity is also an eschewing of personal ambition and over-analysis which can lead to paralysis, anxiety and dilemma. A peaceful life characterized by simplicity in speech, conduct, outlook and lifestyle purifies the mind and draws one closer to God. The Virtue of Simplicity extends to simplicity of worship of, and faith in, God.

"The wisdom of life consists in the elimination of non-essentials" (Lin Yutang). Wisdom resides with those embodying the traits of simplicity. Often the simple and humble acquire wisdom; the educated and learned lack common sense. Therefore declutter your mind, body and life by slowly and gradually letting go of all attachments, illusions and nonessentials. Attune to your inner beauty. And just be your ordinary, natural self, living an ordinary and unpretentious life (*Lin Chi*).

Unless you become like little children, you shall not enter the Kingdom of Heaven (New Testament: Matthew chapter 18 verse 3). Jesus Christ is not exhorting us to behave like little children but rather to reconnect with the loving and open-hearted infant or 'inner child' within each of us, the child who has been slowly but inexorably overwhelmed and silenced by the world and its illusions. Let go of 'adult' conditioned thought and defence mechanisms developed to shield oneself from a sometimes brutal and uncaring world. Search within yourself for your innocent 'child' and childlike qualities – loving, non-judgmental, nondiscriminatory, fearless, open, honest, trusting, joyful, pure and spontaneous – and move towards the Divine.

Scriptural References

Buddhism
Whosoever offends an innocent person, pure and guiltless, their evil comes back upon them like fine dust thrown against the wind.

(The Dhammapada chapter 9 (Evil) verse 125)

Christianity
Except you...become as little children, you shall not enter the Kingdom of Heaven. Whosoever shall humble (oneself) as this little child, the same is greatest in the Kingdom of Heaven.

(Matthew chapter 18 verses 3-4)

Einstein
Out of clutter find simplicity.

(Albert Einstein)

Hinduism
Straightforwardness.

(Saintly Virtue No. 9 of those endowed with a Divine Nature: Bhagavad-Gita chapter 16 verses 1-3)

Judaism
The Law of the Lord is perfect, reviving the soul; the testimony of the Lord is sure (certain), making wise the simple (humble and innocent).

(Psalms chapter 19 verse 7)

The Lord preserves (keeps safe from harm or injury) the simple.

(Psalms chapter 116 verse 6)

Taoism

Manifest plainness. Make excursion in pure simplicity.

(The Domain of Nothingness: Chuang Tzu)

Follow the nature of things.

(Blankness of Mind: Lieh Tzu)

By close attention to the will, compelling gentleness, one can become like a little child.

(Lao Tzu, Tao Te Ching (What is Possible) chapter 10)

Let all…hold to that which is reliable, namely, recognize simplicity.

(Lao Tzu, Tao Te Ching (Return to Simplicity) chapter 19)

Abandon (worldly) cleverness.

(Lao Tzu, Tao Te Ching (Return to Simplicity) chapter 19)

They who (understand themselves)…will come again to the nature of a little child. They who know their innocence and recognize their sin can become the world's model. Being a world's model, infinite *teh* (virtue) will not fail, they will return to the Absolute. They who know the glory of their nature and recognize also their limitations…will revert to simplicity.

(Lao Tzu, Tao Te Ching (Returning to Simplicity) chapter 28)

Simplicity will end desire (attachment and acquisitiveness).

(Lao Tzu, Tao Te Ching (Administering the Government) chapter 37)

The more people are artful and cunning, the more abnormal things occur.

(Lao Tzu, Tao Te Ching (The Habit of Simplicity) chapter 57)

Being simple in actions and in thought, you return to the source of being.

(Lao Tzu, Tao Te Ching (Three Treasures) chapter 67)

Zen Buddhism

Think about what is (really) necessary. Live simply.

(The Zen Manifesto)

Enjoy the small joys that a simple life brings.

(Zen proverb)

Zen is to have the heart and soul of a little child.

(Takuan Soho)

Chapter 34

Study of the Sacred Scriptures

Whatever we conceive God to be and by whatever name we attribute to God, the Divinely-inspired Holy Scriptures reveal the mind of God, the essence of the Divine message or universal precepts, the Law, the Dharma, the Teaching, the Tao, the Way (as the case may be) and the pathway to enlightenment and salvation. Indeed, they contain a veritable repository of spiritual treasures of the heart.

It is through a reading and prayerful contemplation of the Sacred Scriptures that God speaks to the heart of the faithful believer and provides solace, comfort, faith and hope. Study of, and meditation on, the Scriptures and internalizing the word of God in our hearts for practical everyday application, provide nourishment for the intellect, directions along the straight and narrow path, a compass on righteousness and ethical conduct and light for the soul through imparting of Divine wisdom, understanding and spiritual knowledge.

Plant the seed of the Word of God within your spirit and cultivate it well, so that it will sprout forth and produce an abundance of the heart and bountiful good deeds.

Scriptural References

Christianity
Search the Scriptures; for in them you…have eternal life.
(John chapter 5 verse 39)
All Scripture is given by inspiration of God and is profitable for…reproof, for correction, for instruction in righteousness.
(2 Timothy chapter 3 verse 16)
Let the Word of Christ dwell in you richly in all wisdom;

teaching and admonishing one another.

(Colossians chapter 3 verse 16)

Hinduism

Study of the sacred books.

(Saintly Virtue No. 7 of those endowed with a Divine Nature: Bhagavad-Gita chapter 16 verses 1-3)

Islam

(The Qur'an) is the distinction (between right and wrong).

(The Family of Imran chapter 3 verse 4)

Those who are well grounded in knowledge believe in the Scriptures handed down by God.

(The Family of Imran chapter 3 verse 7)

(The Qur'an) is a clear lesson for (humanity) and a guidance and teaching for those who are mindful of God.

(The Family of Imran chapter 3 verse 138)

(The Qur'an) is the path of your Lord leading straight.

(The Cattle chapter 6 verse 126)

God has brought humanity a Scripture explained on the basis of true knowledge – as guidance and mercy for those who believe.

(The Heights (or The Wall with Elevations) chapter 7 verse 52)

As for those who strictly observe (and act on) the Scriptures and are steadfast in prayer, God shall not deny the righteous their reward.

(The Heights (or The Wall with Elevations) chapter 7 verse 170)

When the Qur'an is recited, listen to it and be silent that you may receive mercy.

(The Heights (or The Wall with Elevations) chapter 7 verse 204)

True believers are those...whose faith increases when God's revelations (the Qur'an) are recited to them.

(The Spoils chapter 8 verse 2)

Judaism

This book of (God's) Law shall not depart from your mouth; but you shall meditate therein day and night, that you may observe to do according to all that is written therein: for then you shall make your way prosperous and then you shall have good success.

(Joshua chapter 1 verse 8)

For as the rain and snow come down from the heavens and return not there again, but water the earth and make it bring forth and sprout, that it may give seed to the sower and bread to the eater, so shall My Word (God's Law)...not return to Me void (without producing any effect) but it shall accomplish that which I please and purpose and it shall prosper in the thing for which I sent it.

(Isaiah chapter 55 verses 10-11)

Sikhism

Grant to Thy Sikhs...the gift of reading and understanding the holy Granth Sahib (scriptures).

(Sri Wahguru Ji Ki Fatah!)

Chapter 35

Truthfulness

Unless you become like little children, you shall not enter the Kingdom of Heaven (New Testament: Matthew chapter 18 verse 3).

Young children do not lie but in the course of their upbringing are socialized by society to 'stretch the truth' to gain acceptance and validation and to align with worldly ways. It is indeed very difficult to navigate through this world without at least resorting to some untruthfulness from time to time. But lying distances our souls from the Light.

Truthfulness is honesty; integrity; uprightness; veracity; sincerity; genuineness; good faith; the absence of deceit, slander and lying. Truthfulness is being straightforward and open in all aspects of one's life and not misleading others (particularly in family matters and business relations); not bearing false witness against others, avoiding conjecture and rumor-mongering and restraining oneself from ignoring, not disclosing or manipulating or selectively dealing with the facts to conveniently suit one's purpose or agenda. Although we may sorely be tempted to engage in the euphemistic so-called 'white lie', there is no such thing as an 'innocent' or 'convenient' lie; rather, one should rely on compassionate discretion in knowing or discerning when to speak the truth and knowing when to withhold it (for example, when disclosing it would inflict undue hurt, harm or offence to another in the particular circumstances).

Do not say with your mouth what is not in your heart (Qur'an chapter 3 verse 167). As God is, among other things, Truth, striving to be truthful draws one nearer to God. Being truthful cleanses and purifies the soul.

Scriptural References

Baha'i

Stain not (the tongue) with slander.

(Of Disputation and Fault-Finding: Words of Wisdom from the Supreme Pen of Baha'u'llah)

Be truthful.

(The Commands of the Blessed Master Abdul-Baha)

Buddhism

Abstain from false speech/avoid untruthfulness.

(The Five Precepts and their Meaning: Buddhagosa's Commentary: Papanasudani: Fourth Basic Precept)

Deceit is defilement.

(Sutta Nipata: 2 Kulavagga 2 Amagandhasutta 7 verse 244)

Abstain from speaking falsely.

(Khuddakapatha 2)

They who imagine truth in untruth and see untruth in truth, never arrive at truth, but follow vain desires.

(The Dhammapada chapter 1 (The Twin-Verses) verse 11)

One who acts on truth and virtue is happy in this world and in the next.

(The Dhammapada chapter 13 (The World) verse 168)

Overcome the liar with truth.

(The Dhammapada chapter 17 (Anger) verse 223)

Christianity

There is nothing outside a person that by going in can defile, but the things that come out (of the mouth) are what defile.

(Mark chapter 7 verse 15)

Provide things honest in the sight of all people.

(Romans chapter 12 verse 17)

Put away lying, speak the truth with your neighbor.

(Ephesians chapter 4 verse 25)

Desiderata

Be yourself (sincere/genuine/authentic). Especially do not feign (pretend or imitate deceptively) affection.

(Verses 8-9)

Gandhi

There is no other God than Truth.

(Mohandas Gandhi, *An Autobiography*)

Hinduism

Truthfulness.

(Saintly Virtue No. 11 of those endowed with a Divine Nature: Bhagavad-Gita chapter 16 verses 1-3)

Straightforwardness.

(Saintly Virtue No. 9 of those endowed with a Divine Nature: Bhagavad-Gita chapter 16 verses 1-3)

Islam

Mix not truth with falsehood, nor conceal the truth.

(The Cow chapter 2 verse 42)

Do not say with your mouth what is not in your heart.

(The Family of Imran chapter 3 verse 167)

Those who commit an offence and blame it on an innocent person, shall bear the guilt of calumny (slander) and grievous sin.

(The Women chapter 4 verse 112)

Whenever you give your word, keep your promise.

(The Cattle chapter 6 verse 152)

God loves not the treacherous.

(The Spoils chapter 8 verse 58)

Assumptions can be of no avail against the Truth.

((Prophet) Jonah chapter 10 verse 36)

God verifies the Truth by His Words.

((Prophet) Jonah verse 82)

Give full measure when you measure and weigh with a right (accurate) balance; that is better and fairer.

(The Journey by Night verse 35)

True servants of the Merciful God who bear not false witness shall be recompensed with the highest heaven (ascending heavens).

(The Discrimination chapter 25 verses 72-5)

Believers, fear God and speak the truth. God will bless your good works and forgive you your sins.

(The Confederates chapter 33 verses 70-1)

Do not defame one another.

(The Inner Chambers chapter 49 verse 11)

God raised the heavens on high and set the balance of all things, that you might not transgress that balance. Give just (accurate) weight and full measure.

(The Merciful chapter 55 verses 7-9)

In lofty Paradise there shall neither be harmful speech nor falsehood.

(The Overwhelming chapter 88 verses 10-11)

Woe to every slanderous backbiter (gossiper).

(The Backbiter chapter 104 verse 1)

God is al-Haqq, the Truth.

(The Heights (or The Wall with Elevations) chapter 7 verse 180; Muhammad al-Madani The Ninety-Nine Most Beautiful Names of Allah: No. 18)

The Prophet Muhammad said: "Truthfulness leads to righteousness and righteousness leads to Paradise."

(Sahih Al-Bukhari, 8/6094 (O.P. 116)

Jainism

Deceit is a passion which defiles the soul.

(Sutrakrtanga: Book 1 Sixth Lecture: Praise of Mahavira)

I renounce all lying speech arising from anger or greed or fear or mirth. I shall neither myself speak lies, nor cause others to speak lies, nor consent to the speaking of lies by others.

(Second Great Vow: Acaranga Sutra)

Judaism

You shall not bear false witness against your neighbor.

(The Ten Commandments: Commandment No. 9: Exodus chapter 20 verse 16)

You shall not lie one to another.

(Leviticus chapter 19 verse 11)

You shall not slander.

(Leviticus chapter 19 verse 16)

The Lord hates a lying tongue.

(Proverbs chapter 6 verses 16-17)

A false (inaccurate) balance is abomination to the Lord: but a just (accurate) weight is His delight.

(Proverbs chapter 11 verse 1)

Lying lips are abomination to the Lord: but they who deal truly (honestly) are His delight.

(Proverbs chapter 12 verse 22)

A faithful witness will not lie.

(Proverbs chapter 14 verse 5)

Better are the poor who walk in their integrity, than they who are perverse (false) in their lips and foolish.

(Proverbs chapter 19 verse 1)

A false witness shall not go unpunished and they who speak lies shall not escape.

(Proverbs chapter 19 verse 5)

The just (righteous) walk in their integrity.

(Proverbs chapter 20 verse 7)

Do not deceive with your lips.

(Proverbs chapter 24 verse 28)

Where there is no tale-bearer (slanderer), the strife ceases.

(Proverbs chapter 26 verse 20)

Sikhism

They alone are truly truthful in whose heart is the True One (God) living, whose souls within are rinsed of falsehood...They alone are truly truthful who love truth with a passion.

(Truth as the Heart of Conduct)

Truth is the nostrum (medicine) for all ills. It exorcizes (delivers a person from) sin and washes the body clean.

(Truth as the Heart of Conduct)

Taoism

Rash promises are lacking in good faith.

(Lao Tzu, Tao Te Ching (A Consideration of Beginnings) chapter 63)

The Ten (Native American) Indian Commandments

Be truthful and honest at all times.

(Commandment No. 9)

Zoroastrianism

Truth is best (of all that is good).

(Gathas 27:14)

Speak truth.

(Admonitions)

Commit no slander; so that infamy and wickedness may not happen unto thee.

(Commandments for the Body and the Soul)

The most Holy Spirit joined unto Righteousness; and then did all those who delight to please the Wise Lord (Ahura Mazda (God)) by honest deeds.

(The Primordial Choice: Gatha: Yasna 30)

Chapter 36

Understanding (Knowledge)

Knowledge of the Holy/Divine is understanding (Proverbs chapter 9 verse 10) and those who seek God understand all things (Proverbs chapter 28 verse 5). All Divine knowledge of the unseen is imparted by God to humanity as and when He wills. But how impossible it is for humanity to understand, beyond the most basic and rudimentary level, the spiritual realms, as humanity has been given only a little knowledge thereof by the Creator (Qur'an chapter 17 verse 85). Divine understanding is not the same as human understanding as only the former leads to enlightenment/awakening.

Understanding means comprehension; in this context, deep understanding is the capacity or ability to recognize the Truth, the Dharma or the Tao (as the case may be) through reading and contemplation of the Holy Scriptures, acceptance of reproof and correction and obedience to the Divine Law. Understanding is perceiving the way things actually are as opposed to the way we perceive them to be; observing each phenomenon in its true nature as it actually is, rather than through the prism of material illusion, the attachment of labels or names or through the cultural-religious filter of one's lifelong accumulated individual preconceptions or conditioning. Understanding is knowledge, insight and comprehension of wisdom, the Holy, the Divine. Understanding also extends to comprehending and realizing our highest vision of our soul's potential, supported by the better angels of our nature (self-knowledge/enlightenment). Those who understand themselves are enlightened (Tao Te Ching).

Those who have attained to perfect understanding are silent; they no longer need, or feel the need, to speak. As the saying goes, still waters run deep.

Scriptural References

Baha'i

The root of all knowledge is the knowledge of God...Sow the seeds of My (God's) Innate Wisdom in the pure ground of thy heart and water them with conviction; then the flower of My Knowledge and Wisdom shall spring up verdantly in the holy sanctuary of thy heart.

(Of Knowledge: Words of Wisdom from the Supreme Pen of Baha'u'llah)

Confucianism

The Truth must be genuinely and earnestly realized by each individual.

(Chu tzu ch'uan-shu)

Hinduism

They who know God have left the body behind (abandoned carnal and earthly appetites and desires).

(Svetasvatara Upanisad)

By knowing God one is released from all fetters (attains enlightenment).

(Svetasvatara Upanisad)

Islam

(Humanity) does not comprehend any of God's knowledge except what He pleases.

(The Cow chapter 2 verse 255)

Those who are well grounded in knowledge believe in the Scriptures handed down by God.

(The Family of Imran chapter 3 verse 7)

Such is God's guidance (to the straight path); He bestows it on those of His servants whom He chooses.

(The Cattle chapter 6 verse 88)

We have explained in detail Our (Divine) Revelations (this Qur'an) for a people who understand.

(The Cattle chapter 6 verse 98)

They (the disbelievers) are a people who do not understand.

(The Spoils chapter 8 verse 65)

God guides not those people who are rebellious and work abomination.

(The Repentance chapter 9 verse 80)

The Spirit is one of the things, the knowledge of which is only with God. Humanity has been given only a little knowledge thereof.

(The Journey by Night chapter 17 verse 85)

God has endowed you with hearing, sight and minds (understanding). Little thanks you give.

(The Believers chapter 23 verse 78)

These parables God has put forward for humanity, but none will understand them except those who have knowledge (of God and His signs/revelations).

(The Spider chapter 29 verse 43)

God will exalt those of you who believe and those of you who have been granted (Divine) knowledge.

(The Wrangler chapter 58 verse 11)

God has taught humanity that which it knew not.

(The Clot chapter 96 verse 5)

Jainism

One and eternal is my soul (consciousness), characterized by intuition, insight and knowledge.

(The Lay Person's Inner Voyage: Nityanaimittika-pathavali)

Judaism

The wise will hear and increase in learning (Divine knowledge) and the person of understanding will acquire skill and attain to sound counsel.

(Proverbs chapter 1 verse 5)

Trust in the Lord with all your heart and mind and do not rely on your own understanding. In all your ways acknowledge Him and He will direct and make straight your paths. Be not wise in your own eyes, but reverently fear and worship the Lord.

(Proverbs chapter 3 verses 5-7)

Knowledge of the holy is understanding.

(Proverbs chapter 9 verse 10)

The wise accumulate knowledge of the holy.

(Proverbs chapter 9 verse 14)

Those who love instruction love knowledge.

(Proverbs chapter 12 verse 1)

Knowledge of the holy is easy for one of understanding.

(Proverbs chapter 14 verse 6)

One who is slow to anger is of great understanding.

(Proverbs chapter 14 verse 29)

Wisdom abides in the heart of one of understanding.

(Proverbs chapter 14 verse 33)

One who listens to (and heeds and learns from) reproof (censure or rebuke) acquires understanding.

(Proverbs chapter 15 verse 32)

Those who seek the Lord understand all things.

(Proverbs chapter 28 verse 5)

A good understanding have all they who keep God's Commandments.

(Psalms chapter 111 verse 10)

Sikhism

By hearing the (Divine) Name truth, contentment and Divine knowledge are obtained...By hearing the Name, the unfathomable becomes fathomable...By obeying (God) wisdom and understanding enter the mind. By obeying Him one knows all worlds (seen and unseen).

(The Repetition of the Divine Name: The Japji)

Make Divine knowledge thy food.

(Guru Nanak's Japji)

Make...Divine knowledge thy spiritual guide.

(From the Akal Ustat: Praise of the Immortal)

I have obtained understanding by pondering on Thy (God's) Word.

(Hymn by Guru Angad)

Taoism

Those who have reached the stage of thought (enlightenment, awakening or understanding) are silent. They who have attained to perfect knowledge are also silent.

(Blankness of Mind: Lieh Tzu)

Those who understand themselves are enlightened (awake).

(Lao Tzu, Tao Te Ching (The Virtue (*Teh*) of Discrimination) chapter 33)

Those who know (understand) (The Tao or The Way) do not speak.

(Lao Tzu, Tao Te Ching (The *Teh* of the Mysterious) chapter 56)

The wise are wise because they understand their ignorance and are grieved over it.

(Lao Tzu, Tao Te Ching (The Disease of Knowledge) chapter 71)

Chapter 37

Wisdom

The learned are often not the wise; nor the wise, the learned (Lao Tzu, Tao Te Ching, chapter 81, The Nature of the Essential). The wise learn to be unlearned; they return to that which all others ignore (Lao Tzu, Tao Te Ching, chapter 64, Consider the Insignificant).

Be not wise in your own eyes (Proverbs chapter 3 verse 7) as wisdom is a gift and blessing from God for those who seek and ask for it. Ask, and it shall be given you (New Testament: Luke chapter 11 verse 9). The antithesis of Godly wisdom is ignorance or separation from the Divine Law and Virtues. Wisdom is the ability to discern and properly assess what is true and right (as opposed to what is false and wrong); the ability to appropriately and skillfully utilize Divine knowledge; the willingness to learn by listening to and accepting instruction, correction and counsel from earthly and Divine sources and to learn, and move on, from one's inevitable mistakes. Essentially wisdom is the ability to recognize Truth and to live one's life in accordance with Divine Law.

Wisdom includes qualities of the mind or intellect: prudence, caution, carefulness, discipline, discretion, self-control, humility, keen practical or common sense, sagacity and perspicacity (acuteness or keenness of mental discernment/perception and depth of insight), aversion to evil and sin, and soundness of judgment. Wisdom is acquired and absorbed experientially, not through the mere acquisition of knowledge of facts and skills but rather from distilling Truth from one's life experiences and the Sacred Scriptures and intuitive insights drawn therefrom. Just as peace and contentment come from within, wisdom also comes from within. When we acknowledge the existence of God within us (His immanent quality), our spiritual eye will begin to open and we gradually perceive and understand the Divine Laws and universal energy. Rather than searching for answers without, search your heart within where you will find God and what you seek to know. The Kingdom of God is within you (New Testament: Luke chapter 17 verse 21).

Wisdom also possesses transcendent qualities. Although wisdom is one of the sources or foundations of religion, morality and ethics, it transcends them, extending to a more universal, ultimate and innate way of seeing, perceiving, understanding and being. In its purest form, Wisdom perceives Truth and Love, the only and Ultimate Reality.

Scriptural References

Baha'i
Act with caution and wisdom.

(The Commands of the Blessed Master Abdul-Baha)

Buddhism
By endeavour, earnestness, restraint and control, let the wise make (of themselves) an island that no flood can overwhelm.

(The Dhammapada chapter 2 (On Earnestness) verse 25)

The wise protect their diligence as a supreme treasure. Fools follow after vanity.

(The Dhammapada chapter 2 (On Earnestness) verse 26)

Fools who think themselves wise are called fools indeed.

(The Dhammapada chapter 5 (The Fool) verse 63)

As a solid rock is unshaken by the wind, so are the wise unshaken by praise or blame.

(The Dhammapada chapter 6 (The Wise) verse 81)

Though one may live one hundred years, ignorant and unrestrained, yet better, indeed, is a life of one day for those who are wise and reflecting.

(The Dhammapada chapter 8 (The Thousands) verse 111)

The wise who control their body, who control their tongue, who control their mind, verily, they are fully controlled.

(The Dhammapada chapter 17 (Anger) verse 234)

By degrees, little by little, from moment to moment, the wise remove their own impurities, as a smith blows off the impurities of silver.

(The Dhammapada chapter 18 (Impurity) verse 239)

The wise (person) who, as if holding a pair of scales, chooses what is good and avoids what is evil, is indeed a sage.

(The Dhammapada chapter 19 (The Just) verse 269)

Those who strive not when they should strive, who, though young and strong, are given to idleness, who are loose in their purpose and thoughts, those who are lazy and idle will never find their way to wisdom.

(The Dhammapada chapter 20 (The Way) verse 280)

The highest wisdom lies in not grasping anything as being what it appears to be.

(Atisha)

Christianity

Jesus said, "I thank thee, O Father, Lord of Heaven and earth, because you have hidden these things (Divine knowledge) from the learned and have revealed them unto babes (the simple, humble and innocent)."

(Matthew chapter 11 verse 25)

If any of you lack wisdom, ask of God, Who gives to all generously and it shall be given.

(James chapter 1 verse 5)

Let everyone be swift to hear, slow to speak, slow to wrath.

(James chapter 1 verse 19)

Confucianism

Wisdom, humanity (compassion) and courage, these three are

the universal virtues.

(The Well-Ordered Society: Doctrine of the Mean)

The feeling of right and wrong is the beginning of wisdom.

(The Innateness of the Four Great Virtues: Mencius)

Desiderata

Be careful. Strive to be happy.

(Verses 19-20)

Islam

God gives wisdom (knowledge and understanding) to whomsoever He will, and whoso is given the gift of wisdom (a treasure of the heart) is brought much good. Yet none but those of sense and understanding bear this in mind.

(The Cow chapter 2 verse 269)

The Qur'an is full of wisdom.

(Ya-Sin chapter 36 verse 2)

Jainism

A monk should guard their speech and be possessed of carefulness.

(Sutrakrtanga: Book 1 Tenth Lecture: Carefulness)

As smaller beasts keep at a distance from a lion, being afraid of it, so the wise keep aloof from sin.

(Sutrakrtanga: Book 1 Tenth Lecture: Carefulness)

The wise...knowing the nature of excessive pride and deceit, giving them all up, bring about their liberation. They acquire good qualities and leave off bad qualities.

(Sutrakrtanga: Book 1 Eleventh Lecture: The Path)

Wise, fearless monks consider even a rough instruction (teacher's rebuke) as a benefit, but the fools hate it, though it produces patience and purity of mind.

(Uttaradhyayana: First Lecture: On Discipline)

Guard one's self and never be careless.

(Uttaradhyayana: Fourth Lecture: Impurity)

Judaism

The fear of the Lord is the beginning of wisdom: a good understanding have all they who keep God's Commandments.

(Psalms chapter 111 verse 10)

The Lord gives wisdom: out of His mouth come knowledge and understanding. He lays up sound wisdom for the righteous.

(Proverbs chapter 2 verses 6-7)

Be not wise in your own eyes: fear the Lord and depart from evil.

(Proverbs chapter 3 verse 7)

Do not despise the chastening of the Lord; neither be weary of His correction: For whom the Lord loves He corrects; even as the father the son in whom he delights.

(Proverbs chapter 3 verses 11-12)

Reproofs of instruction (censure or rebuke) are the way of life (character-building/soul-elevating).

(Proverbs chapter 6 verse 23)

Wisdom is better than rubies; and all the things that may be desired are not to be compared to it.

(Proverbs chapter 8 verse 11)

Wisdom dwells with prudence.

(Proverbs chapter 8 verse 12)

Hear instruction and be wise and refuse it not.

(Proverbs chapter 8 verse 33)

Whoever finds wisdom finds life and receives favor from the Lord.

(Proverbs chapter 8 verse 35)

Give instruction to the wise and they will be yet wiser.

(Proverbs chapter 9 verse 9)

The way of a fool is right in their own eyes: but they who heed counsel are wise.

(Proverbs chapter 12 verse 15)

The way of the prudent is to understand one's way (and one's self).

(Proverbs chapter 14 verse 8)

The wise fear, and depart from, evil.

(Proverbs chapter 14 verse 16)

They who (acknowledge and learn from) reproof (censure/rebuke) are prudent.

(Proverbs chapter 15 verse 5)

Fear of the Lord teaches one to be wise.

(Proverbs chapter 15 verse 33)

They who acquire wisdom love (care for or nurture) their own soul.

(Proverbs chapter 19 verse 8)

Hear counsel and receive instruction to acquire wisdom.

(Proverbs chapter 19 verse 20)

The prudent foresee evil and hide from it.

(Proverbs chapter 22 verse 3)

Those who obey the (Divine) law are wise.

(Proverbs chapter 28 verse 7)

Fools utter all their mind: but the wise keep it in till afterwards.

(Proverbs chapter 29 verse 11)

Sikhism

By obeying (God) wisdom and understanding enter the mind; by obeying Him one knows all worlds (the seen and the unseen).

(Guru Nanak's Japji)

Taoism

The wise laugh (are amused) at those with pretensions to power and greatness.

(The Great and the Small: Chuang Tzu)

Prudence and wisdom come to mind when we see great hypocrisy.

(Lao Tzu, Tao Te Ching (The Palliation of the Inferior) chapter 18)

The wise person in all the (varied experiences) of the day will not depart from dignity.

(Lao Tzu, Tao Te Ching (The Virtue (*Teh*) of Dignity) chapter 26)

The wise person to the end will not pose as a great person and by so doing will express their true greatness.

(Lao Tzu, Tao Te Ching (The Perfection of Trust) chapter 34)

The wise live in the world but live cautiously, dealing with the world cautiously.

(Lao Tzu, Tao Te Ching (The Virtue (*Teh*) of Trust) chapter 49)

The wise are inaccessible to favor or hate; they cannot be reached by profit (bribery) or injury; they cannot be honored or humiliated. Thereby the wise are honored by all.

(Lao Tzu, Tao Te Ching (The *Teh* (Virtue) of the Mysterious) chapter 56)

The wise learn to be unlearned; they return to that which all others ignore.

(Lao Tzu, Tao Te Ching (Consider the Insignificant) chapter 64)

The wise discard flattery and prefer regard (respect/ deference).

(Lao Tzu, Tao Te Ching (To Cherish One's Self) chapter 72)

The Ten (Native American) Indian Commandments
Do what you know to be right.
(Commandment No. 6)

Zen Buddhism
The wisdom of life consists in the elimination of non-essentials.
(Lin Yutang)

It takes a wise person to learn from their mistakes, but an even wiser person to learn from others.
(Zen proverb)

Zoroastrianism

With the foolish make no dispute.

(Commandments for the Body and the Soul)

The bee that produces honey has also a sting (enjoining carefulness).

(The Vision of Arda-Viraf)

Chapter 38

Conclusion

36 Divine Virtues or Universal Principles appear to be founded in, and shared across, the following religions and belief systems: Baha'i, Buddhism, Christianity, Confucianism, Hinduism, indigenous spiritual beliefs, Islam, Jainism, Judaism, Sikhism, Taoism and Zoroastrianism. This points to, and indeed is evidence of, the essential core unity of these religions.

As branches grow out from a tree trunk, as droplets of pure monsoon water fall from a lotus blossom and as mighty rivers and tributaries flow out of, and expand from, their original crystal-clear spring-source, these religions have fundamentally evolved from these common underlying spiritual principles. In the course of this evolutionary process, however, religious differences and distinctions have emerged, influenced by the needs and aspirations of the peoples of a particular time and region, and the particular social problems and other circumstances they encountered. Religious prisms have thus reflected the white light of Truth into its spectrum of many different colors and hues. Nevertheless, as is apparent in the preceding pages, a unifying spiritual cord emanating from the One Divine Light and woven through the religious fabric may still be detected, but in these chaotic and confusing times is often overlooked or obscured. Hence, this reminder. If humanity is to evolve and move forward spiritually to a higher consciousness, it must return to the past to rediscover these eternal truths and dynamically apply them today in such a manner as to avert ever increasing existential threats to humanity. To borrow from the Taoist proverb, do not leave the roots to seek the branches. To the root or foundation of all, we must now return. The Single Source of the inspiration for these religions and faiths must be acknowledged, respected and cherished.

In an age when we find ourselves increasingly relying on, and transfixed by, IT devices and social media accounts and burying our faces in our cell phones, and (perhaps unconsciously) allowing our minds and perhaps even our souls to be absorbed into the so-called cyberspace, perhaps it is timely to pause and reflect upon these timeless and eternal Virtues. As knowledge and information exponentially increase, are we losing the ability to utilize them with wisdom and in accordance with these spiritual principles? In order to acquire Godly wisdom and to glean knowledge of the holy and thereby follow the pathway to the ascending heavens, these Divine Virtues must be embraced and internalized and their pristine source rediscovered. To cleanse the downstream waters, the upstream waters must be purified. Therefore cultivate within you an elder's experiential wisdom complemented by a childlike innocence and simplicity. Although the soul may think it is just a drop of water, it is actually the entire ocean.

Our life upon earth is to (re)acquire knowledge of the Divine and of who we truly are before death calls us home. As we navigate our way through the seasons of our earthly existence, the vicissitudes and circumstances thrown up by life and its increasing complexities, the good and the bad, the ups and the downs, we should not be fearful or anxious about the process but rather seize the opportunity to reflect on each of these Divine Virtues and on how we can better apply them in our daily lives. Rather than being confused about the way things *seem* in this world, one may rest content and confident with how they really *are* in the realm of spirit and Truth. What we can see with our eyes is temporary and illusory, worldly and prone to delusion; what we cannot see with our eyes is timeless and eternal. As your life grows shorter with each passing day, seek sanctuary and enlightenment in, and attune your consciousness upon, the realm of spirit and Truth, the timeless and the eternal.

As the French philosopher Pierre Teilhard de Chardin observed, "We are not human beings having a spiritual experience. We are spiritual beings having a human experience." We are much more than our physical bodies. Our true nature is spirit. While everything appears separate and distinct in this earthly realm, everything in the spiritual realm is a part of everything else, as a vibrant intermingled mosaic or tapestry. We are all an interconnected Unity emanating from the Source. This is the Supreme Beatitude.

Scriptural References

Baha'i
Blessed are they who are free; seeking the shore of the Sea of Purity and loving the melody of the dove of Virtue.

(Of Knowledge: Words of Wisdom from the Supreme Pen of Baha'u'llah)

Buddhism
If we wish to die well, we must learn how to live well.

(His Holiness The Dalai Lama)

All conditioned (created) things are impermanent. Work out your own salvation with diligence.

(The Buddha's Last Words)

Christianity
The things which are seen are temporal; but the things which are not seen are eternal.

(2 Corinthians chapter 4 verse 18)

Whatsoever things are true, whatsoever things are honest, whatsoever things are just, whatsoever things are pure…if there be any virtue, and if there be any praise, think on these things.

(Philippians chapter 4 verse 8)

Islam

There is no compulsion in religion; the right path has been distinguished from the wrong path.

(The Cow chapter 2 verse 256)

The greatest bliss is God's good pleasure (Grace). That is the supreme happiness.

(The Repentance chapter 9 verse 72)

(Humanity has) broken up and differed as regards their religion among themselves, but they will all return to Us (God).

(The Prophets chapter 21 verse 93)

Everyone shall taste death. Then to Us (God) you shall be returned.

(The Spider chapter 29 verse 57)

People love the transient life of this world but neglect the Hereafter.

(The Resurrection chapter 75 verses 20-1)

Jainism

Now you have entered on the path from which the thorns have been cleared, the great (and narrow) path...You have crossed the great ocean...Going through the same...practices as perfected saints, you will reach the world of perfection...where there is safety and perfect happiness.

(The Simile of the Leaf: Uttaradhyayana)

Sikhism

All virtues are thine, O Lord; none are mine...There is no devotion without virtue.

(Guru Nanak's Japji)

Human life grows shorter every day...(therefore) arrange your affairs...They whom God awakens and causes to drink the essence of His word, know the story of the Ineffable Embrace for which you have come into the world and God...will dwell in your heart. You shall find a home with comfort and peace in

God's own palace and not return again in this world.

(From the Sohila: Guru Arjan)

Taoism

Matter is necessary to form (a material body is necessary for existence in the earthly realm), but the value (of a life is measured by its immaterial soul).

(Lao Tzu, Tao Te Ching (The Value of Non-Existence) chapter 11)

In olden times the ones who were considered worthy to be called masters were subtle, spiritual, profound, wise. Their thoughts could not be easily understood.

(Lao Tzu, Tao Te Ching (That Which Reveals *Teh* (Virtue)) chapter 15)

All things are in process, rising and returning. Plants come to blossom, but only to return to the root. Returning to the root (God/the Source/the true nature of our soul) is like seeking tranquillity; it is moving towards its destiny. To move towards destiny is like eternity. To know eternity is enlightenment...The decay of the body is not to be feared.

(Lao Tzu, Tao Te Ching (Returning to the Source) chapter 16)

Tao (the Way) is like the brooks and streams in their relation to the great rivers and the ocean (the various religions and faiths).

(Lao Tzu, Tao Te Ching (The Virtue (*Teh*) of Holiness) chapter 32)

They, who dying do not perish, are immortal.

(Lao Tzu, Tao Te Ching (The Virtue (*Teh*) of Discrimination) chapter 33)

Life is a going forth; death is a returning home (to God/the Source).

(Lao Tzu, Tao Te Ching (Esteem Life) chapter 50)

Zen Buddhism

Change how you see and see how you change.

(Zen proverb)

Zoroastrianism

You should not become presumptuous through life; for death comes upon you at last and the perishable part falls to the ground.

(Commandments for the Body and the Soul)

Author Biography

Douglas Hodgson is a dual citizen of Canada and Australia, and a retired lawyer and Dean and Professor of Law residing in Perth, Western Australia. He undertook postgraduate legal study at the University of London before embarking on a 35-year career in higher education in Canada, Australia and New Zealand as a teacher, researcher, scholar, author, human rights advocate and university administrator. His areas of expertise include Public International Law, International Human Rights Law, International Humanitarian Law, Civil Law and Causation Law. Professor Hodgson has authored and published 30 peer-reviewed law journal articles and four books:

The Human Right to Education (Dartmouth/Ashgate, Aldershot, Hampshire, England, 1998)
ISBN: 978-1-85521-909-3

Individual Duty within a Human Rights Discourse (Ashgate, Aldershot, Hampshire, England, 2003)
ISBN: 978-0-7546-2361-8

The Law of Intervening Causation (Ashgate, Aldershot, Hampshire, England, 2008)
ISBN: 978-0-7546-7366-8

International Human Rights and Justice (Nova Science Publishers, Inc., New York, NY, USA, 2016) (Editor)
ISBN: 978-1-63484-709-4

Professor Hodgson's professional networks included the Australian Academy of Law, the Council of Australian Law Deans, the Global Law Deans' Forum and the Australian Research Council. He also served as an advisor to the Australian Red Cross, editor of several law journals and as a member of university human research ethics committees. He is a regular attender and alumnus of the Oxford Round Table where he has delivered addresses on the concept of an international rule of law, the protection of children's international human rights and the challenges of religious fundamentalism in the public school system from a human rights perspective.

As a complement to his work on religious discrimination issues in the educational field, he developed a keen interest in studying and comparing the scriptures of the world's faiths and distilling therefrom common and unifying spiritual principles upon which these great and diverse religions are based, ultimately inspiring him to write *Transcendental Spirituality, Wisdom and Virtue: The Divine Virtues and Treasures of the Heart.*

Bibliography

N. Smart and R. Hecht (eds.) *Sacred Texts of the World: A Universal Anthology* (Quercus Publishing, London, UK, 2007)

M. Borg (ed.) *Jesus and Buddha: The Parallel Sayings* (Duncan Baird Publishers, London, UK, 2008)

S. Kapadia *The Teachings of Zoroaster* (John Murray Publishers, London, UK, 1905)

E. Hammond *The Splendour of God (Extracts from the Sacred Writings of the Baha'is)* (E.P. Dutton and Company, New York, NY, USA, 1909)

D. Field *The Religion of the Sikhs* (John Murray Publishers, London, UK, 1914)

D. Goddard and H. Borel *Laotzu's Tao and Wu Wei* (Brentano's, New York, NY, USA, 1919)

F.M. Muller (translator) *The Dhammapada: A Collection of Verses*, Volume 10, Part I, *The Sacred Books of the East* (Clarendon Press, Oxford, UK, 1881)

E.H. Palmer (translator) *The Qur'an*, Volumes 6 and 9, *The Sacred Books of the East* (Clarendon Press, Oxford, UK, 1880)

H. Jacobi (translator) *Jaina Sutras, The Uttaradhyayana Sutra and The Sutrakritanga Sutra*, Volume 45, Part II, *The Sacred Books of the East* (Clarendon Press, Oxford, UK, 1895)

S. Maher and D. Texidor *The Joy of Zen* (Affirmations Publishing House, Bellingen, NSW, Australia, 2017)

M. Zocchi *The Zen Book of Life* (Brolga Publishing Pty Ltd, Torquay, Victoria, Australia, 2019)

The Holy Bible Containing the Old and New Testaments (King James Version) (Cambridge University Press, London, UK)

Internet Sacred Text Archive (ISTA) http://www.sacred-texts.com

O-BOOKS

SPIRITUALITY

O is a symbol of the world, of oneness and unity; this eye represents knowledge and insight. We publish titles on general spirituality and living a spiritual life. We aim to inform and help you on your own journey in this life.
If you have enjoyed this book, why not tell other readers by posting a review on your preferred book site?

Recent bestsellers from O-Books are:

Heart of Tantric Sex
Diana Richardson
Revealing Eastern secrets of deep love and intimacy to Western couples.
Paperback: 978-1-90381-637-0 ebook: 978-1-84694-637-0

Crystal Prescriptions
The A-Z guide to over 1,200 symptoms and their healing crystals
Judy Hall
The first in the popular series of eight books, this handy little guide is packed as tight as a pill-bottle with crystal remedies for ailments.
Paperback: 978-1-90504-740-6 ebook: 978-1-84694-629-5

Take Me To Truth
Undoing the Ego
Nouk Sanchez, Tomas Vieira
The best-selling step-by-step book on shedding the Ego, using the teachings of *A Course In Miracles*.
Paperback: 978-1-84694-050-7 ebook: 978-1-84694-654-7

The 7 Myths about Love...Actually!
The Journey from your HEAD to the HEART of your SOUL
Mike George
Smashes all the myths about LOVE.
Paperback: 978-1-84694-288-4 ebook: 978-1-84694-682-0

The Holy Spirit's Interpretation of the New Testament
A Course in Understanding and Acceptance
Regina Dawn Akers
Following on from the strength of *A Course In Miracles*, NTI teaches us how to experience the love and oneness of God.
Paperback: 978-1-84694-085-9 ebook: 978-1-78099-083-5

The Message of A Course In Miracles
A translation of the Text in plain language
Elizabeth A. Cronkhite
A translation of *A Course in Miracles* into plain, everyday language for anyone seeking inner peace. The companion volume, *Practicing A Course In Miracles*, offers practical lessons and mentoring.
Paperback: 978-1-84694-319-5 ebook: 978-1-84694-642-4

Your Simple Path
Find Happiness in every step
Ian Tucker
A guide to helping us reconnect with what is really important in
our lives.
Paperback: 978-1-78279-349-6 ebook: 978-1-78279-348-9

365 Days of Wisdom
Daily Messages To Inspire You Through The Year
Dadi Janki
Daily messages which cool the mind, warm the heart and guide
you along your journey.
Paperback: 978-1-84694-863-3 ebook: 978-1-84694-864-0

Body of Wisdom
Women's Spiritual Power and How it Serves
Hilary Hart
Bringing together the dreams and experiences of women across
the world with today's most visionary spiritual teachers.
Paperback: 978-1-78099-696-7 ebook: 978-1-78099-695-0

Dying to Be Free
From Enforced Secrecy to Near Death to True Transformation
Hannah Robinson
After an unexpected accident and near-death experience, Hannah
Robinson found herself radically transforming her life, while a
remarkable new insight altered her relationship with her father, a
practising Catholic priest.
Paperback: 978-1-78535-254-6 ebook: 978-1-78535-255-3

The Ecology of the Soul
A Manual of Peace, Power and Personal Growth for Real People
in the Real World
Aidan Walker
Balance your own inner Ecology of the Soul to regain your
natural state of peace, power and wellbeing.
Paperback: 978-1-78279-850-7 ebook: 978-1-78279-849-1

Not I, Not other than I
The Life and Teachings of Russel Williams
Steve Taylor, Russel Williams
The miraculous life and inspiring teachings of one of the World's
greatest living Sages.
Paperback: 978-1-78279-729-6 ebook: 978-1-78279-728-9

On the Other Side of Love
A woman's unconventional journey towards wisdom
Muriel Maufroy
When life has lost all meaning, what do you do?
Paperback: 978-1-78535-281-2 ebook: 978-1-78535-282-9

Practicing A Course In Miracles
A translation of the Workbook in plain language, with
mentor's notes
Elizabeth A. Cronkhite
The practical second and third volumes of The Plain-Language
A Course In Miracles.
Paperback: 978-1-84694-403-1 ebook: 978-1-78099-072-9

Quantum Bliss
The Quantum Mechanics of Happiness, Abundance, and Health
George S. Mentz
Quantum Bliss is the breakthrough summary of success and
spirituality secrets that customers have been waiting for.
Paperback: 978-1-78535-203-4 ebook: 978-1-78535-204-1

The Upside Down Mountain
Mags MacKean
A must-read for anyone weary of chasing success and happiness
– one woman's inspirational journey swapping the uphill slog for
the downhill slope.
Paperback: 978-1-78535-171-6 ebook: 978-1-78535-172-3

Your Personal Tuning Fork
The Endocrine System
Deborah Bates
Discover your body's health secret, the endocrine system, and
'twang' your way to sustainable health!
Paperback: 978-1-84694-503-8 ebook: 978-1-78099-697-4

Readers of ebooks can buy or view any of these bestsellers by
clicking on the live link in the title. Most titles are published
in paperback and as an ebook. Paperbacks are available in
traditional bookshops. Both print and ebook formats are
available online.
Find more titles and sign up to our readers' newsletter at
http://www.johnhuntpublishing.com/mind-body-spirit
Follow us on Facebook at https://www.facebook.com/OBooks/
and Twitter at https://twitter.com/obooks